Que® Quick Reference Series

AutoCAD®
Quick Reference

2nd Edition

Robert L. Knight
William R. Valaski

Que® Corporation
Carmel, Indiana

AutoCAD Quick Reference, 2nd Edition.

Library of Congress Catalog Number: 90-62954

ISBN 0-88022-622-6

93 92 91   5   4

Interpretation of the printing code: the rightmost double-digit number is the year of the book's printing; the rightmost single-digit number is the number of the book's printing. For example, a printing code of 90-4 shows that the fourth printing of the book occurred in 1990.

This book is based on AutoCAD Release 11. Commands and functions detailed in this book should work with other releases in which the pertinent features are available.

Publishing Director
David P. Ewing

Acquisitions Editor
Terrie Lynn Solomon

Acquisitions Editorial Assistant
Stacey Beheler

Production Editor
Tim Huddleston

Editor
Richard Limacher

Technical Editor
Craig Spaid

Proofreader
Betty Kish

Book Design and Production
Denny Hager, Cindy L. Phipps, Mary Beth
Wakefield

Table of Contents

INTRODUCTION

This command reference is meant to serve as a quick guide for new and experienced AutoCAD users alike. The text covers the commands and functions used within AutoCAD Release 11; it does not cover concepts that may be essential for the effective use of the program. For that type of information, you should refer to a full-featured tutorial book, such as *Using AutoCAD*, 3rd Edition, published by Que Corporation.

This book is divided into three parts. The first part lists each command in alphabetical order and provides a purpose, syntax, and description for each. The second part lists AutoCAD's system variables, each with a brief description. The final part provides you with an abridged listing of the possible responses to each of AutoCAD's commands.

Throughout this book, AutoCAD prompts and messages are displayed in a `different typeface`. An example of this is AutoCAD's `Command:` prompt. Information that you enter is shown in boldface type (such as **Aperture**). Often, when you enter a command, AutoCAD responds by displaying a series of options. Among these options usually is a value enclosed within angular brackets (<>). This value is known as a *default* value — and it typically changes with each command. AutoCAD automatically uses the default value when you press Enter in response to a command prompt.

Some commands, such as Zoom and Pan, can be used *transparently*; that is, you can issue them while another command is in use. To issue a command transparently, precede it with an apostrophe ('). You do not need to add the apostrophe when you are not using the command transparently. To use a command normally, just type the command at the AutoCAD `Command:` prompt. For more information on transparent command usage, refer to the '(Apostrophe) section following the list of commands.

AutoCAD also uses a second "set" of commands.
These commands, called *dimensioning subcommands*,
may only be called from the dimensioning (Dim:)
prompt. These commands relate directly to the
dimensioning of drawing entities.

COMMAND REFERENCE

This Command Reference includes all the AutoCAD
commands, listed in alphabetical order. Each command
is presented in the same format: the command name
appears first, followed by a short explanation of the
command's purpose. The command's syntax is then
shown, along with all the accompanying AutoCAD
propmpts, options, and messages. Finally, the
command's operations and options are described. The
"Description" section contains additional comments,
hints, and suggestions for using the command.

' (Apostrophe)

Identifies the next command as transparent and
instructs AutoCAD to execute the new command
without interrupting the current command.

Syntax

Dim: **'Command**

Description

You can issue a transparent command while another
command is still in progress. The following commands
may be issued transparently:

Ddemodes
Ddlmodes
Ddrmodes
Graphscr
Help or ?
Pan
Redraw
Redrawall
Resume

Setvar
Textscr
View
Zoom

Transparent commands offer you a great deal of
flexibility and power. You can, for example, use a
transparent command to enlarge the display or modify
variables without leaving the command you are
executing. Many experienced users issue the Help
command transparently to obtain information about the
nontransparent command currently in use.

Special features for specific commands are covered
within their command descriptions.

Aligned

Places a dimension line parallel to two selected points.

Syntax

```
Dim: Aligned
First extension line origin or Return
  to select:
Select line, arc, or circle:
Dimension line location:
Dimension text <measured length>:
```

Description

This is a dimensioning subcommand that is available
only from the Dim: prompt. See the descriptions for
Dim and Dim1 for information about dimensioning.

Angular

Measures the angle between two lines.

Syntax

```
Dim: Angular
Select first line:
```

```
Second line:
Enter dimension line arc location:
Dimension text <measured angle>:
Enter text location:
```

Description

This is a dimensioning subcommand that is available only from the `Dim:` prompt. See the descriptions for Dim and Dim1 for information about dimensioning.

If you press Enter at the `Enter text location:` prompt, AutoCAD places the text in the dimension arc. Otherwise, the text appears at the location you indicate. If the text does not fit, AutoCAD displays the following prompt:

```
Text does not fit. Enter new text
    location:
```

Aperture

Controls the size of the aperture box in object snap modes.

Syntax

```
Command: Aperture
Object snap target height (1-50
    pixels) <current>:
```

Description

The size of the aperture box can be changed to fit your preference. The box's size shows AutoCAD how much drawing area to search when you select object snap modes. If you make the size too small, it will be difficult to select endpoints, intersections, and other object snaps of entities. If the aperture is too large, too many entities may reside within the aperture box and the wrong entity may be selected. You may have to try several settings to find the best size, if the standard AutoCAD setting is undesirable.

Arc

Draws an arc segment.

Syntax

```
Command: Arc
Center/<Start point>:
Center/End/<Second point>:
End point:
```

Description

At each prompt, you enter a point. AutoCAD does not recognize a straight line as an arc of infinite radius. If the three points lie on a straight line, AutoCAD displays an error message.

There are several methods for entering points to define an arc. The Center option enables you to indicate the arc's center point. The <Start point> option indicates the arc's starting point, and the End option indicates its end point. The <Second point> option indicates a point along the arc.

The Radius option enables you to enter a radius for the arc. The Direction option prompts you for the arc's tangent direction, and the Angle option prompts you for the arc's included angle. The Length of chord option indicates the arc's chord length.

Area

Calculates the area of an object.

Syntax

```
Command: Area
<First point>/Entity/Add/Subtract:
```

Description

<First point> is the default. You can enter points clockwise or counterclockwise. You do not need to re-enter the first point; AutoCAD automatically "closes" the area. Use the Entity option when you want to find the area of circles and polylines.

The Add option sets add mode and switches between adding and subtracting areas. The prompt changes to:

```
<First point>/Entity/Subtract:
```

As you add and subtract, AutoCAD keeps a running total of the area and displays this total as you work. The Subtract option sets subtract mode.

Array

Makes multiple copies of entities.

Syntax

Rectangular Arrays

```
Command: Array
Select objects:
Rectangular or Polar array (R/P):R
Number of rows (—) <1>:
Number of columns (||||) <1>:
Unit cell or distance between rows
    (—):
Distance between columns (||||):
```

Description

Rectangular arrays are based on horizontal rows and vertical columns. *Unit cell* refers to vertical and horizontal distances between entities. If you indicate opposite corners of the array at the Unit cell prompt, AutoCAD skips the prompt for column distances. Positive values, when entered for the row and column distances, array the objects "up" and "right" across your drawing.

To create a rotated array, use the Snap command's Rotate option, and rotate your snap grid.

Syntax

Polar Arrays

```
Command: Array
Select objects:
Rectangular or Polar (R/P):P
Center point of array:
```

```
Number of items:
Angle to fill (+-CCW, -=CW) <360>:
Angle between items:
Rotate objects as they are copied?
  <Y>:
```

Description

Center point of array: is the point around which all entities are copied.

Number of items: is the number of copies you want.

Angle to fill: is the number of degrees you want these copies to fill.

Angle between items: is the angle that separates the entities in the array.

The last prompt asks if the objects are to be rotated. AutoCAD rotates the objects in accordance with the polar array.

You must provide information for at least two of these three prompts: Number of items:, Angle to fill:, and Angle between items:. If you do not want to give information at a prompt, press Enter and the next prompt appears.

Attdef

Creates an attribute definition that controls various aspects of textual information assigned to a block.

Syntax

```
Command: Attdef
Attribute modes: Invisible:N
  Constant:N Verify:N Preset:N
Enter (ICVP) to change, Return when
  done:
Attribute tag:
Attribute prompt:
Default Attribute value:
Justify/Style/<Start point>:
First text line point:
```

```
Second text line point:
Height <0.20>:
```

If you are working with `Constant` attributes, the following prompt appears (rather than the `Default attribute value:` prompt):

```
Attribute value:
```

Description

`Attribute modes` are settings that control various aspects of the attributes. There are four modes: `Invisible`, `Constant`, `Verify`, and `Preset`. These modes are set for each attribute you assign to a block, and they may be different for each attribute in the block.

`Invisible` mode controls the visibility of the attributes when the block is inserted into the drawing.

`Constant` mode gives attributes a fixed (unchangeable) value.

`Verify` mode simply prompts you for the value you have entered for the attribute, so that you can verify the value.

`Preset` mode enables you to have variable attributes and not be prompted for the value upon insertion of the block.

`Attribute tag:` is the label for the attribute you are defining. All attributes associated with a single block must have different tags. Different blocks may have the same tags for their attributes.

`Attribute prompt:` depends on the setting for `Constant` mode. If the attribute is constant, there is no need for a prompt; the attributes do not change when the block is inserted. If the attributes are variable, the prompt is used when the blocks are inserted. You create this prompt, which appears in the command area to indicate what information the attribute needs. Spaces are accepted as spaces.

`Attribute value:` is the actual piece of information in the attribute. If your attributes are set constant, this information remains the same whenever you insert this particular block.

The remaining prompts are the same as the Text command prompts.

Attdisp

Overrides the default visibility setting for all attributes.

Syntax

```
Command: Attdisp
Normal/On/Off <current setting>:
```

Description

Normal defaults to the setting at which the attributes were created.

On overrides the display settings and turns on all attributes, making them visible. Off overrides the display settings and turns off all attributes, making them invisible.

Attedit

Enables you to edit attributes.

Syntax

```
Command: Attedit
Edit attributes one by one? <Y>:
Block name specification <*>:
Attribute tag specification <*>:
Attribute value specification<*>:
```

Description

At the Edit attributes one by one? <Y>: prompt, you must tell AutoCAD whether you want to edit attributes individually or globally. If you answer Y (for one-by-one editing), you are restricted to the visible attributes. Prompts at each attribute enable you to change the location, angle, height, and other properties as well as the value. You can further limit the attributes edited by selecting certain block names, tags, or values for attributes.

If you answer **N** (for global editing), you are not
restricted to the visible attributes. You can specify the
attributes you want to edit by indicating tag, value, or
block name. When you edit globally, you can change
only the value of the attribute.

After you have selected an editing mode, you need to
specify block names, attribute tags, and attribute
values. Use a comma to separate two or more names.
You may use wild-card characters in the names — the
asterisk (*) for many characters and the question mark
(?) for a single character. Only the attributes you
specify will be edited.

One-by-One Editing

If you are editing attributes one-by-one, the following
prompt appears:

```
Select attributes:
```

The attributes are edited in reverse order (the last
attribute selected is the first attribute you edit). This
attribute is marked with an X, and the following
prompt appears:

```
Value/Position/Height/Angle/Style/
   Layer/Color/Next <N>:
```

The Value option enables you to change the value set
when you originally inserted the block, provided that
the value is not constant. AutoCAD prompts:

```
Change or Replace? <R>:
```

If you select Change, the following prompt appears:

```
String to change:
New string:
```

Type the string you need changed, press Enter, and
then type only the letters that need to be changed.

If you select Replace, AutoCAD prompts:

```
New attribute value:
```

Type the new value and press Enter.

Position enables you to specify a new location for
the attribute.

Height enables you to change the height of the attribute text.

Angle enables you to change the angle for the text.

Style refers to the text font or style used.

Layer enables you to change the layer on which the attribute resides.

Color enables you to change the color for the attributes.

When you finish with one attribute, AutoCAD moves the X to the next attribute to be edited. The same series of prompts is displayed for each attribute.

Global Editing

If you are editing attributes globally, AutoCAD displays the following set of prompts:

```
Global edit of Attribute values.
Edit only Attributes visible on
  screen? <Y>:
```

If you answer Y, AutoCAD prompts you for any block names, tags, or values for restricting the editing of the attributes. The attributes are limited to those visible on-screen.

If you answer N, AutoCAD tells you that the drawing will be regenerated after the editing process and prompts you to select any block names, tags, or values for restriction of the editing process.

After you set the specifications (if any) for the block names, tags, and values, AutoCAD displays the following prompt for editing visible attributes only:

```
Select Attributes:
```

AutoCAD indicates with an X the attribute currently being edited. You are prompted:

```
String to change:
New string:
```

These two prompts appear for each attribute selected, until all the attributes chosen have been edited.

If you edit all the attributes, AutoCAD switches to text mode. You are then prompted:

```
String to change:
New string:
```

AutoCAD searches the attributes you have selected.
The first time it encounters the string to change,
AutoCAD replaces that string and prompts you for a
new string to change. If you press Enter at the
`String to change:` prompt, AutoCAD places the
new string at the beginning of all the attributes. When
you are finished editing, press Enter in response to
both prompts.

Attext

Extracts attribute information from a drawing.

Syntax

```
Command: Attext
CDF, SDF, or DXF Attribute extract
  (or Entities)? <C>:
Template file <default>:
Extract file name <drawing name>:
```

Description

Indicate the form you want the extracted file to take by
using CDF (AutoCAD's Comma-Delimited Format),
SDF (which is similar to dBASE III's SDF format), or
DXF, (AutoCAD's Drawing Interchange File format).
Next, input a `Template file` to tell AutoCAD
how to structure the data in the extract file. (See the
AutoCAD Reference Manual for information on how
to create a template file.)

Finally, enter the name of the file that will receive the
extracted information.

Audit

Verifies the integrity of a drawing file from within the
Drawing Editor.

Syntax

```
Command: Audit
Fix any errors detected? <N>:
```

Description

You can use the Audit command to reconstruct drawing information from a corrupted drawing file. If you answer N to the prompt, AutoCAD informs you of any errors found in the drawing file, and writes that information to an ASCII file for later review.

If you answer Y, AutoCAD fixes any errors it detects in the drawing file.

Axis

Sets up an axis of tick marks on the bottom and right side of the drawing area.

Syntax

```
Command: Axis
Tick spacing (x) or ON/OFF/Snap/
  Aspect <current>:
```

Description

Tick spacing is the default. Type a value at the prompt to set the spacing for both the X and Y axes.

ON turns on the axis after the spacing is set; OFF turns off the axis.

Snap sets the axis to the current snap value.

Aspect enables you to specity different X and Y values for spacing.

Base

Specifies the insertion point of the current drawing when it is inserted as a block into another drawing.

Syntax

```
Command: Base
Base point <current>:
```

Description

The default is 0,0,0, (X,Y,Z) using the World
Coordinate System.

Baseline

Uses the last or previously entered dimension as a base
point for the next dimension to be entered.

Syntax

```
Dim: Baseline
Select base dimension: Dim
Second extension line origin:
Dimension text <value>:
```

Description

This dimensioning subcommand is available only from
the `Dim:` prompt. See the descriptions of the Dim and
Dim1 commands for information about dimensioning.

Note that because AutoCAD uses the first extension
line origin of the last dimension you input as the base
point, you are prompted for the second extension line
origin without being prompted for the first.

Blipmode

Toggles blips on and off.

Syntax

```
Command: Blipmode
ON/OFF <current>:
```

Description

Blips are the small + symbols that AutoCAD inserts
whenever you input a point or select an entity. These
blips disappear after the image is redrawn.

Block

Creates an object from existing entities.

Syntax

```
Command: Block
Block name (or ?):
Insertion base point:
Select objects:
```

Description

Blocks are parts created from objects existing in AutoCAD. To see a list of all the blocks you have created, enter a question mark (?) and press Enter at the first prompt. A complete listing of the blocks currently in the drawing appears on the screen. This list includes user blocks, external references, dependent blocks, and unnamed blocks.

The `Block` name can be 31 characters long and contain letters, numbers, the dollar sign ($), hyphen (-), and underscore(_). AutoCAD converts letters to uppercase. If the block exists, AutoCAD prompts:

```
Block _____ already exists.
Redefine it? <N>:
```

When you redefine a block, be sure not to redefine it to itself; that is, don't take an inserted block and redefine the block to its current name. To redefine a block, redraw the entire block or use the Explode command.

`Insertion base point:` is the reference point AutoCAD uses to pull the part back into the drawing. When you identify the insertion base point, you are prompted to select objects.

Break

Removes parts of an entity or separates an entity into segments.

Syntax

```
Command: Break
```

```
Select object:
Enter second point (or F for First):F
First point:
Second point:
```

Description

In response to the last two prompts, specify two points to define the segment to be removed.

If the two points are on a line or arc, AutoCAD removes the part of the entity that falls between the two points you specify. If one point is beyond the end of the line or arc, that entire part is removed.

If you want to remove a segment from a circle, locate the second point counterclockwise from the first.

You also can break a polyline between two points. If the polyline has a nonzero width, the ends are cut square. If you have fit a curve to the polyline, the information becomes permanent and the polyline can no longer be decurved. The tablet menu features two Break commands: Break and Break @. Break removes a piece from an entity. Break @ separates the entity without removing a piece. If you use Break @, AutoCAD prompts you for a first point. That first point is where the entity will be divided. Note that Break @ will not work on a circle because AutoCAD does not permit arcs to have 360 degrees or more.

Center

Marks the center of a circle or an arc.

Syntax

```
Dim: Center
Select arc or circle:
```

Description

This dimensioning subcommand is available only from the Dim: prompt. See the descriptions of the Dim and Dim1 commands for information about dimensioning.

This subcommand places a graphical cross (+) at the center of the entity you select.

Chamfer

Connects two lines with a new line segment.

Syntax

```
Command: Chamfer
Polyline/Distances/<Select first
  line>:
Select second line:
Enter first chamfer distance
  <current>:
Enter second chamfer distance
  <current>:
```

Description

At the `Polyline/Distance/<Select first line>`: prompt, the distances default to 0. To set these distances to the desired value, type **D** at this prompt. The first distance is applied to the first line you select; the second, to the second line you select. After specifying the distances, repeat the Chamfer command and select the lines.

If you type **P** at the `Polyline/Distance/ <Select first line>`: prompt, AutoCAD enables you to chamfer polylines. Remember, however, that AutoCAD cannot chamfer parallel lines.

Change

Modifies entities.

Syntax

```
Command: Change
Select objects:
Properties/<Change point>:
```

Description

There are two ways to change entities: by indicating a `Change point` or by changing the `Properties`. A change point modifies the physical entity. Properties are color, linetype, layer, and a few other selections.

If you use a change point, your result depends on the type of entity you are modifying.

Line–The end of the line closest to the change point moves to the change point. Several lines may be indicated. Changing a line or group of lines' end points are affected by AutoCAD's Ortho feature.

Circle–The radius is changed so that the circumference passes through the change point.

Text–The location of the text is changed. The insertion point for the text is moved to the change point. If you press Enter at the `Properties/<Change point>:` prompt, AutoCAD prompts for a new text style, text height, rotation angle, and text string. You can change all aspects of text, with some exceptions. If the text is defined with a fixed height, you cannot change the height of that particular font.

Block–You can provide a new insertion point by indicating a change point.

If you select `Properties`, AutoCAD displays the following prompt:

```
Change what property <Color/LAyer/
   LType/Thickness) ?
```

`Color` changes the color of an entity. If you have overridden the layer color and want the entity to default to the layer color, type **BYLAYER**. This tells AutoCAD to set colors by layer. AutoCAD then displays the following prompt:

```
New color <current>:
```

If the current color is BYBLOCK, the entities are set to the color of the block in which they reside. You also can use this setting to override the layer color setting. Select the color (by number or by name) that you want to assign to the entity.

`LType` changes the linetype of the entities. The comments listed under the Linetype command apply here. Again, if you change an entity's linetype, you are overriding the layer setting unless you are changing the linetype to BYLAYER.

`Thickness` modifies the entities' three-dimensional height.

Chprop

Modifies the properties of an entity.

Syntax

```
Command: Chprop
Select objects:
Change what property (Color/LAyer/
  LType/Thickness)?:
```

Description

Chprop is a limited version of the Change command. It will change only the properties of entities. For more information, see the description of the Change command.

Circle

Draws a circle.

Syntax

```
Command: Circle
3P/2P/TTR/<Centerpoint>:
Diameter/<Radius>:
```

Description

3P prompts you for three points. The circle is drawn with its circumference lying on the three points.

2P prompts you for two points. The two points define the circle's location and its diameter.

TTR stands for Tangent/Tangent/Radius. The circle to be drawn is placed tangent to two other entities; you specify the radius.

If you select Centerpoint, you can enter a value for the circle's radius or diameter.

Color

Sets the color of new entities.

Syntax

```
Command: Color
New entity color <current>:
```

Description

You can respond to the prompt by typing the name or the number of the color you want to use to draw an entity.

When you use BYLAYER rather than a specific color, entities take on the color of the layer in which they reside. When you use BYBLOCK, entities take on the color set for the block. The block's color is determined when you create the block.

Continue

Enables you to use the last dimension inserted as a reference for the next dimension.

Syntax

```
Dim: Continue
Second extension line origin:
Dimension text <value>:
```

Description

This dimensioning subcommand is available only from the Dim: prompt. See the descriptions of Dim and Dim1 for information about dimensioning.

The Continue command is similar to the Baseline command. The difference is that Continue uses the second extension line origin of the last dimension as the first extension line origin of the current dimension. This keeps the dimension lines the same distance from the extension lines whenever possible.

Copy

Copies selected objects.

Syntax

```
Command: Copy
Select objects:
  <Base point or displacement>
    /Multiple:
```

Description

Base point provides AutoCAD with a reference from which to act on selected objects.
Displacement enables you to enter a displacement for X, Y, and Z coordinates. If you indicate a Base point or Displacement, AutoCAD displays the following prompt:

```
Second point of displacement:
```

With Base point, indicate the second point. With Displacement, press Enter.

Multiple enables you to make multiple copies at one time. If you select Multiple, AutoCAD prompts you as follows:

```
Base point:
```

This prompt tells you that AutoCAD still needs a reference. With Multiple, you may want the base point to be on the object you are copying. When the base point is on the selected object, copying is easier to calculate. You are then prompted for a location of each new object with:

```
Second point of displacement:
Second point of displacement:
Second point of displacement:
```

AutoCAD enables you to locate as many new copies as you want. When you finish copying the object, press Enter.

Dblist

Lists information about all the entities in a drawing.

Syntax

```
Command: Dblist
```

Description

Dblist stands for *database list*. The information scrolls across the screen. To stop the listing, press Ctrl-S; then press any key to resume. Press Ctrl-C to cancel the command, or Ctrl-Q to echo the command's output to the printer.

Ddatte

Enables attribute editing by means of a dialogue box.

Syntax

```
Command: Ddatte
Select block:
```

Description

This command displays a dialogue box on-screen, so that you can change entity attributes in an interactive fashion.

Ddedit

Enables the user to edit both text and attribute definitions by means of a dialogue box.

Syntax

```
Command: Ddedit
<Select a TEXT or ATTDEF object>
  /Undo:
```

Description

This command displays a dialogue box, so that you can edit text strings in an interactive fashion on-screen.

Ddedit also enables you to modify attribute definitions that already have been created in a block.

Ddemodes

Enables changes in entity creation properties by means of a dialogue box.

Syntax

Command: **Ddemodes**

Description

This command displays a dialogue box, so that you can change entity-creation information in an interactive fashion on-screen. You can use Ddemodes to modify entity properties such as color, linetype, elevation, thickness, and text style.

You can use Ddemodes transparently (by preceding the command with an apostrophe), but any actions taken will not have any effect until the beginning of the *next* command. For more information on transparent commands, see the section on the apostrophe at the beginning of this Command Reference.

Ddlmodes

Enables changes in layer properties by means of a dialogue box.

Syntax

Command: **Ddlmodes**

Description

This command displays a dialogue box so that you can modify the properties of selected layers in an interactive fashion. These properties include layer color, linetype, and state (ON/OFF, Freeze/Thaw), as well as viewport visibility. AutoCAD Release 11 enables you to freeze and thaw layers within viewports.

You can use Ddlmodes transparently, as described in
the section on the apostrophe at the beginning of this
Command Reference.

Ddrmodes

Sets drawing aids by means of a dialogue box.

Syntax

Command: **Ddrmodes**

Description

This command displays a dialogue box, so that you can
change drawing aid properties (such as snap, grid, axis,
ortho, and blips) in an interactive fashion on-screen.

Ddrmodes is yet another command that can be used
transparently. For more information on transparent
commands, see the section on the apostrophe at the
beginning of this Command Reference.

Dducs

Controls the User Coordinate System by means of a
dialogue box.

Syntax

Command: **Dducs**

Description

This command displays a dialogue box, so that you can
define or set the current UCS in an interactive fashion
on-screen.

Delay

Delays execution of the next command in a script.

```
Command: Delay
Delay time in milliseconds:
```

Description

Delay is used in developing AutoCAD scripts. The command enables you to specify, in milliseconds, the amount of time to delay before returning control either to the user or to the next command in the script.

Diameter

Provides diameter dimensions.

Syntax

```
Dim: Diameter
Select arc or circle:
Dimension text <measured diameter>:
```

Description

This dimensioning subcommand is available only from the Dim: prompt. See the descriptions of Dim and Dim1 for information about dimensioning.

The point at which you select the arc or circle determines where the dimension appears.

Dim or Dim1

Sets dimensioning mode.

Syntax

```
Command: Dim
or
Command: Dim1
```

Description

Dim1 enables you to enter only one dimension and then returns you to the Command: prompt. The Dim command, on the other hand, places you in dimensioning mode so that you can execute several dimensioning subcommands. You can issue the following dimensioning subcommands at the `Dim:` prompt:

Aligned	Leader	Save
Angular	Newtext	Status
Baseline	Oblique	Style
Center	Override	Tedit
Continue	Radius	Trotate
Diameter	Redraw	Undo
Exit	Restore	Update
Hometext	Rotate	Vertical
Horizontal		

Modification to AutoCAD's dimensioning features was one of the major enhancements of Release 11. Now, dimension entities not only retain their *associative quality*, but can be altered more easily. This associative feature (that is, the dimension values' capability to update themselves automatically as you edit the drawing) has existed since Version 2.6 (Release 8).

The largest drawback to associative dimensioning was the user's inability to edit the dimension's appearance. New features, however, give the user such abilities. One such feature (Trotate) enables you to rotate the text string. Another permits you to position the text anywhere for better readability (the Tedit command).

For detailed information about each of these dimensioning subcommands, see the appropriate command descriptions.

To return to the `Command:` prompt after using the Dim command, type **Exit** at the `Dim:` prompt, or press Ctrl-C.

═Dist

Calculates the distance between two points.

Syntax

```
Command: Dist
First point:
```

```
Second point:
Distance = <calculated distance>
Angle in X-Y plane = <angle>
Angle from X-Y plane = <angle>
Delta X = <X change> Delta Y = <Y
   change> Delta Z = <Z change>
```

Description

Distance calculates the three-dimensional distance between two points. Distance displays the following values: distance and angle in the X-Y plane, angle from the X-Y plane, and delta values for X, Y, and Z planes.

Divide

Divides an entity into equal parts.

Syntax

```
Command: Divide
Select object to divide:
<Number of segments>/Block:
```

Description

If you specify the number of segments into which the entity should be divided, AutoCAD uses point entities to mark the division points on the object to be divided. If you select Block, AutoCAD prompts as follows:

```
Block name to insert:
Align block with object <Y>:
Number of segments:
```

The specified block will be located along the object at the division points.

Donut or Doughnut

A special polyline command that creates rings of variable width.

Syntax

```
Command: Donut  or Doughnut
Inside diameter:
Outside diameter:
Center of doughnut:
Center of doughnut:
```

Description

Inside diameter is the donut's inside diameter.
For solid filled circles, set the inside diameter to 0.

Outside diameter is the donut's outside
diameter.

The Center of doughnut: option enables you to
enter as many doughnuts as you need with a single
command.

Dragmode

Determines the display of objects and their new
locations while editing is taking place.

Syntax

```
Command: Dragmode
ON/OFF/Auto <current>:
```

Description

The ON option permits dragging when appropriate. The
OFF option disables all dragging. If you select the
Auto option, all commands that support dragging will
drag.

When you work with complex or many objects, your
computer might appear slow as it displays each
possible editing outcome. If this occurs, it may be less
time-consuming to turn Dragmode off until you have
finished.

Dtext

Displays text on-screen as it is typed at the keyboard.

Syntax

```
Command: Dtext
Justify/style/<Start point>:
First text line point:
Second text line point:
Height <0.20>:
Text:
```

Description

The difference between the Dtext and Text commands
is that Dtext echoes the text on-screen as you type, and
enables you to create multiple lines of text.

Dtext displays the same prompts as the Text command,
and all Dtext selections have the same meaning as do
Text selections. When you use any of the justification
options, you must finish typing your text and press
Enter before AutoCAD can adjust the text on the
display.

Dview

Displays parallel or perspective views.

Syntax

```
Command: Dview
Select objects:
CAmera/TArget/Distance/POints/PAn/
   Zoom/TWist/CLip/Hide/Undo/ <eXit>:
```

Description

Dview enables you to choose the exact location and
angle of the view for a three-dimensional model. This
occurs dynamically; that is, the view is temporarily
displayed as you answer the second prompt. Once you
have the view you like, exit from the command and the
view is displayed.

You begin by selecting the objects to view. Often it
will be your entire model, but your computer will
operate much faster if you select only the objects you
want to see. An example might be to select only a
building entrance rather than the entire building.
Should you want to use your entire drawing, press

Enter at the `Select objects:` prompt. AutoCAD
displays a graphical house to aid you in determining
your view. After you decide on the view, choose
`exit`; the house disappears and your model is
displayed.

The options for determining your Dview begin with
`Camera`, which pulls up the slider bars. You can
change the angle from which you are viewing the
drawing, either by using the slider bars or by typing in
the new angle. The camera is rotated around the target.

`TArget` enables you to change the target (that is, the
object you are viewing). The target is rotated around
the camera.

`Distance` changes the distance between the camera
and the target. This option turns on the perspective
view.

`POints` enables location of both camera and target
using X, Y, and Z coordinates. The target point is
specified first, and then the default target is located in
the center of the viewport on the current UCS X-Y
plane.

`PAn` operates in the same fasion as the standard Pan
command, but is dynamic.

`Zoom` enables you to adjust the camera's lens length if
perspective is on. If perspective is off, you have a
standard zoom center. The default lens length is
approximately 50mm, which provides the same view
as a "normal" lens on a 35mm camera.

`TWist` enables you to tilt or twist the view around the
line of sight. (This command uses a camera-target
setup to define the line of sight.)

`CLip` enables you to define clipping planes. This is
how you define cutaways in your drawing. You should
note that these clipping planes are placed perpendicular
to the line of sight. AutoCAD blanks whatever is in
front of the front clipping plane or whatever is behind
the back clipping plane. You receive the following
prompt:

    `Back/Front/<Off>:`

`Back` blocks objects behind the back clipping plane.
The following prompt appears:

```
ON/OFF/distance from target
  <current>:
```

Front blocks objects between you (the camera) and the front clipping plane. The following prompt appears:

```
ON/OFF/Eye/distance from target
  <current>:
```

If Eye is selected, the clipping plane is positioned at the camera.

Off turns off perspective view; use Distance to turn on perspective.

Hide removes hidden lines from the currently selected entities.

Undo undoes the last Dview option executed. If you use more than one option, you can step back through the whole command.

eXit ends the Dview command.

Dxbin

Loads compacted binary files, such as those produced by AutoShade.

Syntax

```
Command: Dxbin
File name:
```

Description

After executing Dxbin, enter the name of the binary file you want to load. For a more detailed description of this file, see the *AutoCAD Reference Manual*.

Dxfin

Loads files saved in the DXF (drawing interchange file) format.

Syntax

```
Command: Dxfin
File name:
```

Description

Enter an empty or new drawing to load an entire DXF file to ensure that any layering, blocks, linetypes, text styles, and so on are generated correctly. If you are working in a drawing that already has these elements, only entity information is loaded.

Dxfout

Writes the current drawing file to a drawing interchange file or a binary file.

Syntax

```
Command: Dxfout
File name <default>:
Enter decimal places of accuracy
  (0 to 16)/Entities/Binary <6>:
```

Description

Enter the name of the file that will receive the drawing information. The `Enter decimal places of accuracy` prompt defines the accuracy of the stored information. You can indicate specific `Entities` to be written, or you can specify a `Binary` file.

Edgesurf

Constructs a Coons surface patch, which is a polygon mesh bounded on four sides by entities you select.

Syntax

```
Command: Edgesurf
Select edge 1:
Select edge 2:
Select edge 3:
Select edge 4:
```

Description

A *Coons surface patch* resembles a fishing net. This "net" can be wavy or flat, but it is basically developed in two directions. These directions are determined by the edges selected. Edges may be lines, arcs, or open polylines—and must connect end to end.

The two directions of the net are called the *M* and *N* directions. The M direction is determined by the first entity you indicate, while the N direction is determined by the two entities connected to the first.

Elev

Controls the location of the current X-Y construction plane on the Z axis.

Syntax

```
Command: Elev
New current elevation <current>:
New current thickness <current>:
```

Description

Elev controls where the current X-Y construction plane is located along the Z axis. Subsequently drawn entities can extrude above or below the construction plane (thickness).

Ellipse

Draws ellipses.

Syntax

```
Command: Ellipse
<Axis endpoint 1>/Center:
Axis endpoint 2:
<Other axis distance>/Rotation:
```

or

```
Command: Ellipse
<Axis endpoint 1>/Center: C
Center of ellipse:
Axis endpoint:
<Other axis distance>/Rotation:
```

Description

In the *Syntax* section, the default set of prompts is
shown first. The second set of prompts appears if you
use the Center option.

To draw ellipses, AutoCAD uses both major and minor
axes. AutoCAD uses the axes' length to set up the
ellipse. The default prompt asks you to indicate one
axis, and then the endpoint for the other axis.
AutoCAD looks for a distance to apply to the second
axis. If the second axis is shorter than half the length of
the first, AutoCAD uses the first axis as the major axis.
If, however, this distance is longer, the first axis
chosen will become the minor axis of the ellipse.

The second way to draw ellipses involves entering the
center point for the ellipse. AutoCAD then prompts
you for a point to define one of the axes. The next
prompt asks for the endpoint of the second axis. The
last prompt line has another selection—Rotation.
Using the first axis as the major axis, AutoCAD rotates
the ellipse around that axis.

End

Saves your drawing and returns you to the Main Menu.

Syntax

Command: **End**

Description

End is similar in purpose to the Quit command. Issue
the End command to exit from the Drawing Editor,
save the drawing's contents, and return to the
AutoCAD Main Menu.

Erase

Removes entities from the drawing.

Syntax

```
Command: Erase
Select objects:
Select objects:
```

Description

After you issue the Erase command, simply select the objects you want to erase. At the second prompt, press Enter to execute the command.

Exit

Returns you to the Command: prompt from the Dim command.

Syntax

```
Dim: Exit
```

Description

This dimensioning subcommand is available only from the Dim: prompt. See the descriptions for Dim and Dim1 for information about dimensioning.

Use Exit when you want to leave dimensioning mode and return to the AutoCAD Command: prompt. You can get the same result by pressing Ctrl-C.

Explode

Separates a block or polyline into its original entities.

Syntax

```
Command: Explode
Select block reference, polyline,
dimension or mesh:
```

Description

Select the block you want to break apart. Special color or layer assignments no longer exist. All entities are moved to layer 0 and become white.

When you need to modify a block, you must explode, modify, and then redefine the block. You cannot modify a block that has been inserted with different X, Y, or Z values; nor can you explode a block with negative insertion factors.

Extend

Extends entities to a boundary.

Syntax

```
Command: Extend
Select boundary edge(s)...
Select objects:
<select object to extend>/Undo:
```

Description

The entity or entities to be extended must be visible on-screen, and you must specify a boundary to which the entities can be extended. The first two prompts ask for the boundaries to which you want to extend the affected entities. After you select the boundaries, press Enter. AutoCAD then prompts you to select the object to extend. You can choose the Undo option to undo the last extend performed.

Files

Enables you to perform limited system operations while still in the AutoCAD Drawing Editor.

Syntax

```
Command: Files
```

Description

The Files command enables you to list, delete, rename, copy, and unlock files without exiting from the Drawing Editor. The command lets you perform these file-related functions through a menu.

Fill

Controls the solid fill of polylines and solids.

Syntax

```
Command: Fill
ON/OFF <current>:
```

Description

If Fill is on, objects are filled with color; if Fill is off, only the entities' outlines appear on-screen.

Fillet

Trims or extends two entities or places a fillet radius between them.

Syntax

```
Command: Fillet
Polyline/Radius/<Select two objects>:
```

Description

This command connects the end points of lines or polylines. As such, each line is either extended or trimmed to a point at which they both meet. The Fillet command can also be used to place an arc of a specific radius between the lines or polyline. When you select Polyline at the prompt, AutoCAD asks for the polyline to fillet. The command modifies all segments that are long enough to be filleted.

The default Radius is 0. Filleting entities with this radius causes them to be trimmed or extended to a sharp corner. To change the radius, type **R** at the prompt. AutoCAD prompts for the new radius:

```
Enter fillet radius <current>:
```

After you enter the radius, AutoCAD ends the Fillet
command and returns you to the `Command:` prompt.
The radius you entered remains in effect until you
change it.

Filmroll

Generates a file used for rendering, if you are using
AutoShade.

Syntax

```
Command: Filmroll
Enter the filmroll file name
  <default>:
```

Description

When you execute this command, AutoCAD creates a
filmroll file for the rendering program AutoShade.

Graphscr

Switches a single-screen system from text display to
graphics display.

Syntax

```
Command: Graphscr
```

Description

This command switches the screen from text to
graphics (Drawing Editor) mode, which is just the
opposite of the Textscr command.

Graphscr can be used transparently. That is, it may be
used within another command. For more information
on transparent commands, see the discussion of the
apostrophe at the beginning of this Command
Reference.

Grid

Sets up a rectangular array of reference points within the drawing limits.

Syntax

Command: **Grid**
Grid spacing (x) or ON/OFF/Snap/
  Aspect<current>:

Description

Grid spacing is the default and sets both the X and the Y value for the grid. If you enter a value and press Enter, the grid automatically turns on at your setting.

When the grid is set up, you can toggle it on and off by means of the ON and OFF options. You also can toggle the grid on and off by pressing F7 or Ctrl-G.

By default, the grid setting is equal to the snap setting. If you want your grid to default to the snap setting, use the Snap option. Aspect is used to set differing X and Y values for the grid. You are prompted separately for the X value first, and then for the Y value. Remember to respond to both prompts.

Because the points on grids are not drawing entities, you cannot reference them physically.

When you are working with the grid on, AutoCAD may display a Grid is too dense error message. This message means that, because the grid points are too close together to show on-screen, AutoCAD cannot place the grid. If this happens, reset the grid to a larger value.

Handles

Controls the system variable that establishes unique identifiers for entities.

Syntax

Command: **Handles**
ON/DESTROY:

Description

Handles are identifiers or tags associated with every entity in the drawing. Handles enable third-party applications to do estimating or quantity take-offs automatically from your drawing.

ON is the default. This tells AutoCAD that all entities have a handle defined.

DESTROY deletes all entity handles in the drawing. Because this option is potentially dangerous, AutoCAD displays a special message. To destroy the handles, you must enter a special phrase.

Hatch

Performs hatching.

Syntax

```
Command: Hatch
Pattern (? or name/U,style)
  <default>:
Scale for pattern <default>:
Angle for pattern <default>:
Select objects:
```

Description

The ? option displays a listing of available hatch patterns.

When you want to change the hatching style, type the name of the pattern followed by a comma and the first letter of the style type: N for normal, O for outermost, or I for ignore. The default style is normal.

U,style enables you to describe your own pattern. You are prompted for the angle for the lines, the spacing between the lines, and whether you want the area double-hatched, as follows:

```
Angle for crosshatch lines
  <default>:
Spacing between lines <default>:
Double hatch area? <default>:
```

Scale enables you to change the hatch pattern's scale. You may have to experiment to find the best scale for your drawing.

All hatch patterns are created in reference to the X axis. If you want to hatch a rotated object, and you want the pattern to align with the object, enter the rotation angle at the Angle for pattern <default>: prompt.

Help or ?

Provides on-line documentation.

Syntax
Command: **Help** or **?**
Command name (Return for list):

Description
If you enter a command at the Command name (Return for list): prompt, AutoCAD displays information about that command. If you press Enter at the prompt, AutoCAD displays a listing of all commands, as well as some general program information. To use Help transparently while another command is executing, place an apostrophe before the command.

Hide

Removes hidden lines.

Syntax
Command: **Hide**

Description
Based on database information, AutoCAD determines which lines in your drawing should be hidden (behind other entities) and then redraws the screen with those lines removed. This command may take some time to use if your drawing is large.

Hometext

Returns dimension text to its home position.

Syntax

```
Dim: Hometext
Select objects:
```

Description

This dimensioning subcommand is available only from the Dim: prompt. See the descriptions of the Dim and Dim1 commands for information about dimensioning.

Associative dimension text has a default location, called its "home" position. This subcommand returns associative dimension text to its original position if it has been moved.

Horizontal

Places the horizontal (X) distance between two points.

Syntax

```
Dim: Horizontal
First extension line origin or Return
  to select:
Second extension line origin:
Dimension line location:
Dimension text <value>:
```

Description

This dimensioning subcommand is available only from the Dim: prompt. See the descriptions of the Dim and Dim1 commands for information about dimensioning.

Id

Displays the coordinates of a point on-screen.

Syntax

```
Command: Id
Point:
```

Description

The specified point does not have to be located on an entity. You can use object snap modes to snap onto parts of entities to define specific points.

Igesin

Converts and loads files in Initial Graphics Exchange Standard (IGES) format.

Syntax

```
Command: Igesin
File name <current>:
```

Description

The IGES format enables you to transfer drawings between AutoCAD and other CAD packages. The IGES file by itself is unusable as an AutoCAD drawing file. Once brought into a new drawing with the Igesin command, however, the file becomes a usable drawing.

Igesout

Saves the current drawing to Initial Graphics Exchange Standard (IGES) format.

Syntax

```
Command: Igesout
File name <current>:
```

Description

The IGES format enables you to transfer files between AutoCAD and other CAD packages. When you use Igesout to save the file in IGES format, the newly saved file is no longer in usable AutoCAD form. To return an IGES file to AutoCAD form, use the Igesin

command. Note that your original drawing file will not
be altered; this command only creates a new file.

Insert

Places a block or an entire drawing at a specified
location in the current drawing.

Syntax

```
Command: Insert
Block name (or ?):
Insertion point:
X scale factor <1>/Corner/XYZ:
Y scale factor <default=X>:
Rotation angle <0>:
```

Description

At the Block name (or ?): prompt, type the
name of the block you want to insert. With Release 11,
if you type a tilde (~) character, a dialogue box
appears, listing the available blocks to insert.

Insertion point: prompts you for the location
of the block. This is the point that will be aligned with
the insertion base point you defined when you created
the block.

At the X scale factor <1>/Corner/XYZ:
prompt, you can enter a number or a point, or you can
press Enter if you want the block inserted at the scale
drawn. If you enter a point, you can drag a second
point to give AutoCAD the X and Y scales at the same
time. The default value for the scale factor is 1. This
value causes the block to be inserted at the scale at
which it was drawn.

At the Y scale factor <default=X>:
prompt, you can enter a Y-scale factor that is different
from the X-scale factor. If you want the X-scale factor
to be the same as the Y-scale factor, press Enter.

Negative scale values are acceptable, but blocks with
negatives scale values cannot be exploded. A negative
X value mirrors the block around the Y axis; a negative
Y value mirrors the block around the X axis. With the

`Rotation angle <0>:` prompt, the block is rotated around the insertion point at the given angle. If you accept the default angle of 0, the block is inserted at the orientation created. Angle input is applied counterclockwise.

Isoplane

Changes the orientation of the crosshairs when you are working in isometrics.

Syntax

```
Command: Isoplane
Left/Top/Right/(Toggle):
```

Description

The Isoplane command acts as a toggle; to change between the different settings, simply press Enter at the prompt or press Ctrl-E. When drawing isometrically, this command enables you to switch between the three most commonly used drawing planes (30°, 60°, and 90°).

Layer

Creates and modifies layers.

Syntax

```
Command: Layer
?/Make/Set/New/ON/OFF/Color/Ltype/
  Freeze/Thaw:
```

Description

The `?` option displays a list of layers and their status.

`Make` is a combination of the `Set` and `New` options. When you use `Make`, AutoCAD asks which layer you want to be the current layer. AutoCAD searches for the layer name. If it is not found, AutoCAD creates a new layer with that name and sets that layer.

Use the Set option to identify the layer on which you want to draw.

New creates new layers. You are prompted for the layer names. To enter more than one layer name at a time, type the name followed by a command and the next name.

ON turns on layers. When you create a new layer, it defaults to on. OFF turns off layers. When layers are off, you cannot see the entities, if any, that exist on those layers.

Color enables you to set the layer color. AutoCAD can produce 255 colors. You will be limited, however, if your graphics card and monitor cannot produce that many colors. The default color for new layers is white. Setting the color also defines the color of the entities that reside on a given layer.

Ltype sets the linetype for the layer. The default is the solid linetype.

You can save time in your work by using the Freeze option to freeze layers. When you freeze a layer, AutoCAD ignores the entities on that layer. As a result, AutoCAD can regenerate the drawing much more quickly.

Thaw lets you access frozen layers. AutoCAD automatically turns on thawed layers. Both Thaw and Freeze require AutoCAD to regenerate the drawing.

Leader

Enables you to place notes in a drawing.

Syntax

```
Dim: Leader
Leader start point:
To point:
To point:
Dimension text <last dimension
  entered>:
```

Description

This dimensioning subcommand is available only from the Dim: prompt. See the descriptions of the Dim and Dim1 commands for information about dimensioning.

Respond to the To point: prompts as you would for a normal Line command. You can undo Leader segments if you want. When you finish entering end points, press Enter. AutoCAD then prompts you for the text you want to insert. The default text is the last dimension entered in AutoCAD. Unlike Text or Dtext, Leader limits you to one line of text.

Limits

Controls drawing size.

Syntax

```
Command: Limits
ON/OFF/<LLC> <current value>:
Upper right corner <12.00,9.00>:
```

Description

ON engages the limits check, which is a beep that warns if you go outside the drawing's boundaries.

LLC is the lower left corner of the drawing area. The default (0,0) is the standard setting for Limits. You can press Enter to accept 0,0 as the lower left corner, or you can enter a point by either digitizing or typing the X and Y values.

Upper right corner <12.00,9.00>: is the drawing's upper right corner. Remember that the X (horizontal) value comes first, followed by the Y (vertical) value.

Line

Draws a straight line.

Syntax

```
Command: Line
From point:
To point:
To point:
```

Description

The From point: prompt asks you for the starting
point of the first line segment.

The To point: prompt asks you for the end of the
current line segment. The point you specify at this
prompt is used as the beginning for the next line
segment. If you press Enter without entering a point,
the Line command ends.

If you type U at the To point: prompt, AutoCAD
undoes the last line segment drawn. If you remain in
the Line command while you undo the segment,
AutoCAD enables you to pick up the line segments at
the previous point entered.

If you type C at the prompt, AutoCAD automatically
closes the sequence of lines. You must have two or
more line segments to use the Line command's close
option.

Linetype

Creates, loads, and sets linetypes.

Syntax

```
Command: Linetype
?/Create/Load/Set:
```

Description

The ? option lists the linetypes available in a linetype
file. If you select the ? option, AutoCAD displays the
following prompt:

```
File to list <acad>:
```

Enter the name of the file containing the linetypes you
want to view. AutoCAD then returns you to the
Linetype prompt.

`Create` enables you to create linetypes.

If a linetype is in a file other than ACAD.LIN, you must use the `Load` option to load it. If you select `Load`, the following prompt appears:

```
Name of linetype to load:
File to search <default>:
```

The `Set` option sets the linetype with which you will be working. All the entities you draw from this point will be drawn in the linetype you set. If you draw a block with some entities set to the layer's default linetype (some with linetype overrides, and some set to linetype by block), there will be confusion when the block is inserted. Some entities will retain the linetype you want, and other entities will change to the layer default. You are prompted as follows:

```
New entity linetype <current>:
```

As with all overrides, be careful about changing the entities in your drawing. Use the overrides with caution.

You can override the linetype for entities in the same fashion as the colors, by using either the Change or Chprop commands.

List

Lists information about entities in a drawing.

Syntax

```
Command: List
Select objects:
```

Description

Information listed about one or more entities consists of layer, values, coordinates, size, font and style (if text), or area (if a closed polyline). Generally, AutoCAD provides a great deal of information, which varies with each type of entity. To echo the information to your printer, press Ctrl-Q before pressing Enter at the `Select objects:` prompt.

Load

Loads compiled shape and font files.

Syntax

```
Command: Load
Name of shape file to load (or ?):
```

Description

Only shape files that have been successfully compiled at the Main Menu can be loaded.

Ltscale

Changes the scale of linetypes in the drawing.

Syntax

```
Command: Ltscale
New scale factor <default>:
```

Description

Enter a value greater than 0 for the scale. The default for new drawings is 1. You may have to set the scale a few times to get the correct spacing on your linetypes. You may need to set the value to between 100 and 200 before the linetype is readable in the drawing.

Measure

Measures a distance, placing points or markers at intervals.

Syntax

```
Command: Measure
Select object to measure:
<Segment length>Block:
```

Description

The Measure command is similar to the Divide command, with one exception. Divide is used to place a specified number of points along an entity at *equal distances* from each other. Measure places points along an entity at a *specified distance* from each other.

Begin by selecting the object you want to measure. Type the length or **B** (for Block). The length is measured from the end of the entity nearest the point at which you selected that entity. If you are using the Block option, AutoCAD prompts:

```
Block name to insert:
Align block with object? <Y>:
Segment length:
```

Measure can use only a block that has been created and is already in the drawing.

Menu

Enables you to work with menus other than the standard AutoCAD menu.

Syntax

```
Command: Menu
Menu file name or . for none
  <current>:
```

Description

Enter the name of the new menu you want to use. AutoCAD supports screen menus, button menus, tablet menus, and pull-down menus.

The standard AutoCAD menu is the software that works with the plastic digitizer template. The Menu command enables you to run another menu. Other menus are supplied by third-party vendors, or you can develop your own special menus.

Minsert

Inserts a block more than one time.

Syntax

```
Command: Minsert
Block name <or ?):
Insertion point:
X scale factor <1>/Corner/XYZ:
Y scale factor <default = X>:
Rotation angle <0>:
```

Description

These are the standard Insert prompts; see the Insert
command for an explanation of the options. The only
difference between Insert and Minsert is that you
cannot enter a block name with an asterisk (*) to insert
an exploded block. Following the insertion prompts,
AutoCAD prompts you to array the newly inserted
block. This feature is similar to a *rectangular array*.
The prompts for the array section of the Minsert
command appear as follows:

```
Number of rows (---) <1>:
Number of columns (||||) <1>:
```

Type the number of rows and the number of columns.
If the number of rows is greater than 1, AutoCAD
prompts for the distance between the rows or for a unit
cell:

```
Unit cell or distance between
  rows (---)
```

A unit cell includes both the block and the distance
between the rows. .

Mirror

Reflects entities on an axis.

Syntax

```
Command: Mirror
Select objects:
First point of mirror line:
Second point:
Delete old objects? <N>:
```

Description

You begin the Mirror operation by selecting the objects with which you want to work. Because the *mirror line* is the line of symmetry in the final object, its placement is important. At the next two prompts, specify the first and second points that define this line.

You can keep the original entities or delete them by responding appropriately to the Delete old objects? <N>: prompt.

Move

Moves entities in the drawing.

Syntax

```
Command: Move
Select objects:
Base point or displacement:
Second point of displacement:
```

Description

When you specify a base point, you give AutoCAD a reference for moving the selected entity. This is equivalent to the insertion base point for blocks.

You also can specify a displacement for the entity, rather than a second point; for example, you can specify that the object be moved 2' 6" directly to the right by typing @2'6"<00. You must enter at least an X and Y value; AutoCAD accepts X, Y, and Z values.

No matter how you respond to the previous prompt, AutoCAD then prompts for a second point. If you entered a displacement, press Enter in response to this prompt. If you indicated a base point, either "show" AutoCAD where you want the entities by dragging them, or indicate the coordinates for the second point.

Mslide

Creates a slide from the current screen image.

Syntax

```
Command: Mslide
Slide file <default>:
```

Description

Before you execute the Mslide command, load the
drawing into the Drawing Editor and zoom in on the
area that you want to be the slide. When you issue
the Mslide command, AutoCAD prompts for the name
of the slide file. Name the file according to your
operating system's file-name conventions. AutoCAD
creates the slide from the screen's contents.

Mspace

Switches from paper space to model space.

Syntax

```
Command: Mspace
```

Description

This command switches the current viewport to model
space. You first must use the Mview command to
define the model viewports.

Multiple

Repeats another command until canceled.

Syntax

```
Command: Multiple <Command>
```

Description

If you issue Multiple together with another AutoCAD
command, the command repeats itself until you press
Ctrl-C. For example, if you want to place several lines
consecutively, type **Multiple Line** at the `Command:`
prompt. The Multiple command causes the Line
command to keep repeating until you terminate it.

Mview

Treats viewports as entities.

Syntax

```
Command: Mview
Switching to Paper space.
ON/OFF/Hideplot/Fit/2/3/4/Restore/
   <First Point>:
```

Description

This command works in conjunction with the Vports (or Viewports) command to create and manipulate the drawing's viewports.

The ON and OFF options toggle the display of model space in the individual viewports in order to speed up the moving and resizing of the viewports.

If you select the Hideplot option, AutoCAD asks if you want lines in the viewport to be hidden when the drawing is plotted in paper space; the request appears as ON/OFF:. This option does not affect the display. To remove hidden entities from the view, use the Hide command.

To enlarge the viewport so that it fills the available display area, use the Fit option. The display area is dependent upon the paper space view's size. The viewport in which this command is used becomes the current viewport.

If you select the 2, 3, or 4 option, you choose the number of viewports to be displayed on-screen. When you choose one of these numbers, AutoCAD asks how you want to divide the screen.

The Restore option enables you to reconstruct a viewport configuration, saved with the Vports command, within paper space.

Fit lets you scale any restored viewports within the current graphics area.

First Point enables you to define a viewport by specifying two of its corners.

Newtext

Enables you to change the text in an existing associative dimension.

Syntax

```
Dim: Newtext
Enter new dimension text:
Select objects:
```

Description

This dimensioning subcommand enables you to change the text string in an associative dimension. Newtext can be issued only at the Dim: prompt. For more information on dimensioning, see the descriptions of the Dim and Dim1 commands.

Oblique

Enables dimension leader lines to be set at an oblique angle.

Syntax

```
Dim: Oblique
Select objects:
```

Description

Typically, leader lines are inserted perpendicular to the dimension. If these lines interfere with the readability of the drawing, you can use the Oblique command to adjust their positions. You must use Oblique at the Dim: prompt. For more information on dimensioning, see the descriptions of the Dim and Dim1 commands.

Offset

Creates a new entity that is parallel to the original.

Syntax

```
Command: Offset
Offset distance or Through <last>:
```

Description

If you specify an `Offset distance`, all offsets will be that distance. The following set of prompts appears:

```
Select object to offset:
Side to offset:
```

First select the entity to be offset, and then specify a point on the side of that entity on which you want to place the offset.

If you select `Through`, AutoCAD prompts for the point through which the new entity will pass. The following prompts appear for each entity:

```
Select object to offset:
Through point:
```

AutoCAD is looking for the entity to offset and the point through which the new entity must pass.

Oops

Brings back the last group of entities erased.

Syntax

```
Command: Oops
```

Description

Similar in purpose to the Undo or U commands, Oops enables you to undo or negate your previous edits.

Ortho

Restricts you to horizontal or vertical movement of the cursor.

Syntax

```
Command: Ortho
ON/OFF:
```

Description

Press Enter at the prompt to toggle Ortho on or off.
You also can toggle Ortho by pressing F8 or Ctrl-O.

Osnap

Sets global object snap modes.

Syntax

```
Command: Osnap
Object snap modes:
```

Description

Object snap modes can be used globally, with the
Osnap command, or individually. If the mode is set
globally, it is invoked whenever AutoCAD looks for
point information. To use the object snap modes
selectively, type in the appropriate mode at the prompt
for point information, and press Enter. AutoCAD
prompts for the entity with which you want to work.

You can indicate modes by typing just the first three
letters of the mode name. You can choose from the
following modes:

NEArest   Locates a point visually nearest the
             crosshairs on the entity and snaps to
             that point.

ENDpoint   Locates the closest endpoint of a line
             or arc, or the closest defining point of a
             solid or three-dimensional face.
             ENDpoint selects the extruded points
             of these entities.

MIDpoint   Snaps to the middle point of a line, arc,
             polyline segment, and the extruded
             sides of an entity. You can apply this
             mode to solids and three-dimensional
             faces as well. This is done by chosing
             the midpoint between the two nearest
             corners.

CENter   Snaps to the center of an arc or a circle.
                  When using this mode, you must
                  indicate the entity by digitizing the
                  circumference. AutoCAD locates the
                  center; you simply indicate the entity
                  with which you want to work.

NODe   Selects a point entity.

QUAdrant   Picks the closest point on a circle or arc
                  at 0, 90, 180, or 270 degrees. You can
                  use this mode only with entities that
                  are in the current UCS, or whose
                  extrusion direction is parallel to the
                  Z axis of the current UCS.

INTersection   Snaps to an intersection only if it is a
                  true intersection in three-dimensional
                  space. For extruded entities, you can
                  select the intersection of the entity and
                  the extrusion lines. If two entities
                  intersect on a UCS and extrude in the
                  same direction, AutoCAD can locate
                  the intersection of the extruded edges.
                  If there is a difference in the amount of
                  extrusion, the shorter extrusion defines
                  the intersection. Make sure that both
                  entities are in the aperture when you
                  indicate the intersection.

INSert   Locates the insertion points of a block,
                  text, or a shape.

PERpendicular Chooses an existing entity so that the
                  new entity is perpendicular to the last
                  point entered on the existing entity.
                  Any extrusion must be parallel to the
                  current UCS Z axis. This mode is used
                  in reference to the last point entered.

TANgent   Selects a point on an entity that is
                  tangent to the last point entered. Any
                  extrusion must be parallel to the
                  current UCS Z axis.

NONe   Cancels any globally set object snap
                  modes. Simply type **NONe** at the
                  `Object snap modes:` prompt and
                  press Enter.

Override

Permits you to alter the value of default dimension variables.

Syntax

```
Dim: Override
Dimension variable to override:
Current value <(the variable's value)> New
  value:
Select objects:
```

Description

Use the Override command to modify one or more of the dimension variables' default values and update any dimension strings accordingly.

When the `Dimension variable to override:` prompt appears, enter the name of the variable. The prompt appears again after you enter the new value. This prompting cycle enables you to alter more than one variable before continuing. To exit the cycle of modifying these values, press Enter at this point. The `Select objects:` prompt then appears, so that you can begin entity selection.

If you choose a dimension that references a named dimension style, the following prompt appears:

```
Modify dimension style "(style
  name)"? <N>:
```

Answer **Y** if you want to update the aspects of that style, as well as the dimension just selected. Answer **N** if you do not want to modify the style's variable settings, but only the dimension. Note that if you answer **Y** here, existing entities that use that style name will not be altered, but any future dimensions will exhibit the new values.

This dimensioning subcommand is available only from the `Dim:` prompt. See the descriptions of the Dim and Dim1 commands for more information about dimensioning.

Pan

Enables you to move around in the drawing without changing the zoom factor.

Syntax

```
Command: Pan
Displacement:
Second point:
```

Description

Pan needs two points. The first is a reference point; the second indicates the direction and distance you want to pan.

You can use Pan transparently; that is, you can issue Pan while another command is executing, by preceding Pan with an apostrophe ('Pan). You cannot, however, use Pan transparently if the current command is Vpoint, Dview, Zoom, Pan, or View. Further, you cannot use Pan transparently if you are working in paper space. Finally, if a the requested 'Pan requires AutoCAD to regenerate the image, the 'Pan will not be carried out. For more information on transparent commands, see the discussion of the apostrophe at the beginning of this Command Reference.

Pedit – 2-D, 3-D

Enables you to edit polylines or meshes.

Syntax

```
Command: Pedit
Select polyline:
```

Description

If the entity you indicate is not a polyline, AutoCAD prompts:

```
Entity selected is not a polyline.
Do you want it to turn into one?
 <Y>:
```

Answer **Y** to turn the entity into a polyline. AutoCAD then displays the following prompt:

```
Close/Join/Width/Edit vertex/Fit
   curve/Spline curve/Decurve/Undo/
   eXit <X>:
```

If the selected polyline is not closed, you can close it with the Close option. If the polyline is closed, the Close option becomes the Open option, and you have the option of opening the polyline.

Join attaches separate line and arc segments to one another, forming a polyline.

Width sets a uniform width for the entire polyline.

When you select the Fit curve option, AutoCAD fits a curve to the polyline. The curves are drawn to tangent points and pass through vertices.

Spline curve is different from Fit curve. A spline is a best-fit curve to the polyline. This selection uses the vertices of the polyline as a frame to draw the spline. The more vertices there are, the more the curve will be "pulled" along the direction of the frame.

Decurve removes the fit curve or the spline from the polyline.

Undo undoes each previous Pedit operation you performed. You can use it to step back to the beginning of the Pedit editing session.

To keep any changes you have made, you must use the eXit option to exit from the Pedit command.

Edit vertex lets you edit individual segments by using the vertices. When you enter this selection, an X appears at the start of the polyline. The X indicates the segment you are using. When you select Edit vertex, AutoCAD displays the following prompt:

```
Next/Previous/Break/Insert/Move/
   REgen/Straighten/ Tangent/Width/
   eXit <N>:
```

Next moves the indicator to the next vertex.

Previous moves the indicator to the previous vertex.

Break removes a segment of the polyline or breaks the polyline into separate entities. If you select the Break option, the following prompt appears:

    Next/Previous/Go/eXit <N>:

Next and Previous move the indicator. The command is executed for the segments you cross while at this prompt. Go executes the selection, and eXit leaves the selection without executing.

Insert puts a new vertex between the current vertex and the next vertex. Move the cursor to the vertex directly before the new vertex, and then select Insert.

Move relocates the current vertex to a specified location.

REgen acts like the normal Regen command. After you change a segment's width, you must use REgen in order to see your changes.

Straighten removes all vertices between two indicated vertices. The Straighten option also displays the Next/Previous/Go/eXit <N>: prompt.

Tangent provides the polyline tangent information used in Fit curve. You can define the angle to which you want the fitted curves to be tangent. Simply move to the vertex and enter the tangent angle. An indicator appears on-screen. Width enables you to change the width of individual segments. You must use Regen to see the change in the width. AutoCAD prompts for both a new beginning width and a new ending width.

eXit returns you to the basic Pedit prompt.

After you change the polyline, you can use other editing commands on it. You can copy, move, erase, array, mirror, rotate, and scale the polyline. If you use these commands, the spline retains its frame. If you break, trim, or explode the polyline, however, the spline frame is deleted. The Offset command creates a polyline fit to the spline.

Pedit (Meshes)

Enables you to edit polylines or meshes.

Syntax

Command: **Pedit**

Description

The following lists show how the Pedit command options react with a three-dimensional polygon mesh:

Decurve	Restores the original mesh
Edit Vertex	Edits the mesh vertexes individually
M	Opens or closes the mesh in the M direction (the length of the mesh)
N	Opens or closes the mesh in the N direction (the width of the mesh)
S	Fits a smooth surface, using the SURFTYPE system variable

The following options are used for vertex editing:

D	Moves down in the M direction to the previous vertex
L	Moves left in the N direction to the previous vertex
M	Moves the indicated vertex
R	Moves right in the N direction to the next vertex
RE	Redisplays the mesh
U	Moves up in the M direction to the next vertex

Pface

Generates a polygon mesh of arbitrary topology, not necessarily composed of four-sided faces.

Syntax

```
Command: Pface
Vertex 1: (Enter X, Y, and Z coordinates of a
    vertex)
Vertex 2:
.
.
.
Vertex n: (Press Enter)
Face 1, vertex 1: (Enter "corner" of the face
    with the number from above)
Face 1, vertex 2:
.
.
.
Face 1, vertex n: (Press Enter)
Face 2, vertex 1: (Enter "corner" of this
    face)
Face 2, vertex 2:
.
.
.
Face 2, vertex n: (Press Enter)
Face 3, vertex 1: (Press Enter to stop)
```

Description

You can use this command to create complicated
meshes. The meshes are complicated because
AutoCAD accepts an unlimited number of vertices and
faces. As shown above, each face can have many more
than four sides. This is where the Pface goes beyond
the limits of the 3Dface command (see 3Dface).

Like other AutoCAD mesh patterns, a Pface mesh can
be edited with most of the basic editing commands,
including Array, Chprop, Copy, Erase, Explode, List,
Mirror, Move, Rotate, Scale, and Stretch. If you want
to make an edge of a face invisible, use a minus sign
(–) before the first vertex number of that edge:

```
Face 1, vertex 3: –3
```
This specification makes the edge of Face 1, which
goes from vertex 3 to vertex 4, but cannot be
seen.

Because it is so complex, this command is most often used by applications software or AutoLISP programs to generate mesh patterns.

Plan

Provides a plan view of the drawing relative to the current UCS, a specified UCS, or the World Coordinate System.

Syntax

```
Command: Plan
<Current UCS>/UCS/World:
```

Description

The Current UCS option provides the plan view with respect to the current User Coordinate System (UCS). If you select the UCS option, AutoCAD prompts for the name of the previously saved UCS for which you want a plan view. You can enter a question mark (?) for a listing of the currently defined UCSs. (For a more detailed discussion of the User Coordinate System, see the description of the UCS command.)

The World option regenerates the drawing to a plan view of the World Coordinates.

Pline

Draws polylines.

Syntax

```
Command: Pline
From point:
Current line width is ___
Arc/Close/Halfwidth/Length/Undo/
  Width/<Endpoint of line>:
```

Description

When you issue the Pline command, you first must specify a starting point from which AutoCAD can

draw the polyline's segments. Indicate a starting point
at the From point: prompt.

The default drawing segment is a line. You can select
the Endpoint of line: option or another option.

If you choose Arc, the following prompt appears:

```
Angle/CEnter/CLose/Direction/
    Halfwidth/Line/Radius/Second pt/
    Undo/Width/<Endpoint of arc>:
```

You now can draw arc segments in any of several
ways. You can use the Angle, CEnter,
Direction, Radius, and Second pt options as
you would with the Arc command.

Close closes the current polyline.

Halfwidth enables you to specify half the width of a
wide polyline. You are prompted as follows:

```
Starting half-width <current>:
Ending half-width <current>:
```

Length enables you to enter the length of the
segment. The segment is drawn at the same angle as
the last segment.

Use Undo to undo the last part of the Pline command.
Undo in Pline reacts the same as Undo in the Line
command.

Width lets you assign widths to polyline segments.

Endpoint is the default; this option tells AutoCAD
to look for the end of the line segment.

Plot

Plots a drawing on a pen plotter.

Syntax

```
Command: Plot
What to plot - Display, Extents,
    Limits, View, or Window <D>:
```

Description

Display plots the current display; that is, the part of the drawing displayed on-screen when the command is executed.

Extents plots the extents of the drawing. Before you plot extents, zoom out to the drawing's extents. If any entities lie beyond the drawing limits, they are included in the extents.

Limits plots the entities that are within the limits you set up for your drawing.

View plots a defined view saved with the View command. Use this for plotting various areas of a drawing.

Window plots an area that you "window." AutoCAD first prompts for two corners of the window.

After you specify the portion of the drawing to be plotted, AutoCAD displays a series of prompts showing you the plot size, origin, pen width, and other information about the plot. You can accept or modify these settings before plotting. The following paragraphs describe these prompts.

The Do you want to change anything? <N>: prompt is where you set the speed of your plotting, pen numbers for layers, and linetypes. The pen numbers are related to the colors of the entities. If you want to change any of the settings for the pens, type **Y** at the prompt. You are prompted for the pen number, linetype, and pen speed for entity color 1. You can respond to these prompts in five ways.

After you enter the changes for the pens, AutoCAD prompts for basic plotting specifications.

With the Write the plot to a file? <Y> prompt, you can send plots to a file rather than the plotter.

You can work in inches or millimeters. The Size units (Inches or Millimeters) <current>: prompt lets you change the size units.

Regarding the Plot origin in units <default X, Y>: prompt, with pen plotters the origin is usually the lower left corner of the paper. This is the home position for the pen. For printer plotters, home is the upper left corner. The plot origin corresponds to the lower left corner of the drawing. AutoCAD lets you move the plot origin. If you are working with D-size paper, you can plot four A-size drawings on the same paper by moving the plot origin.

With the `Enter the Size or Width, Height (in units) <default>:` prompt, AutoCAD enables entry of the plotting area with which you want to work. The maximum plotting size depends on the plotter's size. Plotting size is measured from the plot origin. You can create a margin around the drawing by setting a new plot origin.

The `Rotate 2D plots 90 degrees clockwise? <N>` prompt enables you to rotate the plot 90 degrees. This means that the point that would have been in the lower left corner is now in the upper left corner; all other corners are rotated accordingly.

If you use wide polylines and solids, you may want to adjust the pen width at the `Pen width <default>:` prompt. This affects the amount of work necessary to fill in these areas.

The `Adjust area fill boundaries for pen width? <N>` prompt lets you adjust the plotting of wide polylines and solids by half a pen width. This adjustment provides a more accurate plot.

When you are plotting three-dimensional objects, you can remove the hidden lines by typing **Y** at the `Remove hidden lines? <N>` prompt.

With the `Specify scale by entering:` prompt, you can set the plot's scale. This scale is independent of the drawing scale. You can scale either the drawing or the plot.

Point

Inserts point entities into the drawing.

Syntax

```
Command: Point
Point:
```

Description

You can indicate point locations in any fashion. You can use object snap modes, absolute coordinates, or relative coordinates.

Polygon

Draws a polygon, which is a multisided figure composed of polyline vertices of equal length.

Syntax

```
Command: Polygon
Number of sides:
Edge/<Center of polygon>:
```

Description

When you select the Center of polygon option, you are prompted:

```
Inscribed in circle/Circumscribed
   about circle (I/C):
Radius of circle:
```

Enter I or C and then the radius of the circle.

If you select the Edge option, you are indicating one side of the polygon, not the center point and radius. You are prompted:

```
First endpoint of edge:
Second endpoint of edge:
```

These prompts ask for two points to define one side of the polygon.

Prplot

Sends a plot to a printer that accepts graphics information.

Syntax

```
Command: Prplot
```

```
What to plot - Display, Extents,
   Limits, View, or Window <D>:
```

Description

See the options for the Plot command.

Pspace

Switches from model space to paper space.

Syntax

Command: **Pspace**

Description

This command is used to switch the current viewport
to paper space. The Pspace command has no options.

Purge

Cleans up the drawing database by removing unused
entities.

Syntax

```
Command: Purge
Purge unused Blocks/Dimstyles/LAyers/
   LTypes/SHapes/STyles/All:
```

Description

You can purge unused blocks, layers, linetypes,
shapes, and styles. The All option searches the
database for all unused named objects and presents
them for purging.

This command must be used before you change
(including adding entities to, or removing them from)
the database.

Layer 0, the continuous linetype, and the standard text
style are basic to the drawing and cannot be purged.

Because blocks may reference dimstyles, layers,
linetypes, shapes, and styles, you may want to purge

blocks first. This is not necessary, however, if you use
the All option.

Qtext

Replaces text with a box.

Syntax

```
Command: Qtext
ON/OFF <current>:
```

Description

Qtext is a time-saver for large drawings containing a
great deal of text. Qtext replaces the text with a box.
The text is still in the database but does not regenerate
on-screen.

Quit

Ends the editing session and returns to the Main Menu
without saving changes to the drawing.

Syntax

```
Command: Quit
Really want to discard all changes to
  drawing?
```

Description

Quit is similar in purpose to the End command. Use
Quit to end a drawing session (without saving any
changes made to the drawing during the session) and
return to the main AutoCAD menu.

Radius

Provides radius dimensions for circles and arcs.

Syntax

```
Dim: Radius
Select arc or circle:
Dimension text <measured radius>:
Enter leader length for text:
```

Description

This dimensioning subcommand is available only from the Dim: prompt. See the descriptions of the Dim and Dim1 commands for more information about dimensioning.

The dimension's location depends on the point at which you select the entity.

Redefine

Enables you to reset, to its original definition, a standard AutoCAD command that is currently being handled by a customized LISP routine.

Syntax

```
Command: Redefine
Command name:
```

Description

At the Command name: prompt, enter the name of the command that has been defined to a LISP routine. The command is reset to its original definition.

Redo

Reverses an Undo command.

Syntax

```
Command: Redo
```

Description

This command must be used immediately after the U or Undo command; otherwise it will not work.

Redraw

Redraws entities in the current viewport.

Syntax

Command: **Redraw**

Description

Redraw redisplays all entities on-screen. This is useful should you erase one entity which is on top of another entity; the underlying entity cannot be seen until Redraw or Regen is issued.

Redraw can be used transparently; simply put an apostrophe before the command at any prompt. (For more information about transparent commands, see the discussion of the apostrophe at the beginning of this Command Reference.) Redraw also can be issued at the Dim: prompt. See the descriptions of the Dim and Dim1 commands for information about dimensioning.

Redrawall

Redraws all the viewports at one time.

Syntax

Command: **Redrawall**

Description

Redrawall functions exactly the same as Redraw. Redrawall, however, affects all the current viewports at once. Redraw only redraws the image in the active viewport.

Like Redraw, Redrawall can be used transparently.

Regen

Regenerates the drawing for the current viewport.

Syntax

Command: **Regen**

Description

When you issue Regen, AutoCAD reads the entire
entity database and calculates a new drawing. This
command may be slow to execute if the drawing
contains a large number of entities. This command is
similar in effect to Redraw. If Redraw does not display
the expected image, issue Regen.

Regenall

Regenerates all viewports.

Syntax

Command: **Regenall**

Description

Regenall functions exactly the same as Regen.
Regenall, however, affects all the current viewports at
once. Regen regenerates only the image in the current
viewport.

Regenauto

Limits automatic regeneration.

Syntax

Command: **Regenauto**
ON/OFF:

Description

ON enables automatic regeneration. OFF disables
automatic regeneration. (AutoCAD asks if regeneration
should occur.)

Rename

Renames entities.

Syntax

```
Command: Rename
Block/Dimstyle/LAyer/LType/Style/Ucs/
  VIew/VPort:
Old (object) name:
New (object) name:
```

Description

At the `Block/Dimstyle/LAyer/LType/Style/Ucs/VIew/VPort:` prompt, enter the type of entity you want to rename. Then enter the entity's current name at the `Old (object) name:` prompt, and the new name at the `New (object) name:` prompt.

Restore

Returns altered dimensions' variables to a previously saved set of values.

Syntax

```
Dim: Restore
Current dimension style:
?/Enter dimension style name or
  Return to select dimension:
```

Description

This dimension subcommand works in conjunction with the Save dimension subcommand. If you enter ? at the second response, AutoCAD prompts:

```
Dimension style(s) to list <*>:
```

At this point, you can type a style name or press Enter and see a listing of all the saved dimension styles. If you want to see the differences between the current style and an existing style, precede the style name at this prompt with a tilde (~), such as: ~style1

This subcommand, like the other dimension subcommands, must be entered at the `Dim:` prompt. (See the descriptions of the Dim and Dim1 commands for more information on dimensioning.)

Resume

Continues an interrupted script file.

Syntax

`Command: `**Resume**

Description

You can interrupt a script's execution by pressing Backspace. If you decide to continue the script, enter **Resume** at the `Command:` prompt. If the script stopped while performing a command, you can precede the Resume command with an apostrophe to make the Resume command transparent to the current operation. For more information on transparent commands, see the discussion of the apostrophe at the beginning of this Command Reference.

Revsurf

Generates a surface of revolution by rotating a profile around an axis.

Syntax

```
Command: Revsurf
Select path curve:
Select axis of revolution:
Start angel <0>:
Included angle (+=ccw, -=cw) <Full
  circle>:
```

Description

The `Select path curve:` prompt asks for the outline of the object you are drawing. This object, which can be a line, arc, circle, or two-dimensional polyline, is the N direction of the resulting mesh.

At the `Select axis of revolution:` prompt,
specify the axis around which the path curve revolves.
This axis, which can be a line or an open polyline, is
the M direction of the resulting mesh.

`Start angle <0>:` enables you to begin the
surface at an offset from the defined path curve.

`Included angle (+=ccw, -=cw) <Full
circle>:` specifies how far the entities are rotated
around the axis.

Rotate

Rotates the entities in a drawing.

Syntax

```
Command: Rotate
Select objects:
Base point:
<Rotation angle>/Reference:
```

Description

At the `Select objects:` prompt, specify the point
around which the entities will rotate.

`Base point:` prompts for a point around which the
objects will be rotated.

`Rotation angle` prompts for an angle through
which the entities will be rotated. For example, if you
enter **90**, the objects are turned up on their sides.

`Reference:` enables you to reference an entity in the
drawing as the current angle and then tell AutoCAD
the new rotation. To do this, indicate the ends of the
source entity, using object snap modes if necessary.
Then type the angle to which you want the entities
rotated.

Rotated

Sets a rotation angle for the dimension line.

Syntax

```
Dim: Rotated
Dimension line angle <0>:
First extension line origin or Return
  to select:
Second extension line origin:
Dimension line location:
Dimension text <1.19>:
```

Description

If you are dimensioning a part that is not horizontal or vertical and you cannot align the dimension, use the Rotated linear dimension. This dimensioning subcommand is available only from the Dim: prompt. See the descriptions of the Dim and Dim1 commands for information about dimensioning.

Rscript

Reruns a script file.

Syntax

```
Command: Rscript
```

Description

Rscript is similar in purpose to the Script command. Use Rscript to run a script file an additional time from within the Drawing Editor.

Rulesurf

Creates a ruled surface between two curves, lines, points, arcs, circles, or polylines.

Syntax

```
Command: Rulesurf
Select first defining curve:
Select second defining curve:
```

Description

You can think of defining curves as the ruled surface's boundaries. If one of the boundaries is closed, the other also must be closed. AutoCAD starts the surface from the endpoint of the entity nearest the point used to select the entity. With circles the start is 0 degrees; with polygons the start is the first vertex.

Save

Saves the changes you have made to the drawing, without returning to the Main Menu.

Syntax

```
Command: Save
```

Description

You should save your work every 10 to 20 minutes, depending on how much time you can afford to spend reconstructing a drawing if you happen to lose everything you did since your last "save."

Save (Dim subcommand)

Retains the current dimension variable settings in a style name.

Syntax

```
Dim: Save
?/Name for new dimension style:
```

Description

If you have altered the dimension variables for a certain application within a drawing, you can save the settings so that they can be restored later. You can use any name to save the dimension style. This saved dimension style is located in the current drawing only. It may be retrieved later with the Restore dimensioning subcommand. If you choose a name that already exists, AutoCAD prompts:

```
That name already in use, redefine
   it? <N>
```

If you answer **Y** to this prompt, you do not modify
existing dimension entities in your drawing—only
future dimensions.

The Save dimensioning subcommand works in
conjunction with the Restore dimensioning
subcommand. Do not confuse this Save command with
AutoCAD's Save command, which you use to save
your drawing. For more information on dimensioning,
see the Dim and Dim1 commands.

Scale

Scales specified entities to a new size.

Syntax

```
Command: Scale
Select objects:
Base point:
<Scale factor>/Reference:
```

Description

Use this command to enlarge objects. If you have a
one-inch-diameter gear, for example, and want to place
a two-inch gear beside it, copy the gear and then scale
the new image with the Scale command. After you
select the object to be scaled, specify a base point.
Then you can either indicate the scale factor, or
reference part of the object.

At the Select objects: prompt, select the
entities you want to scale.

Base point is the point from which the entities will
be scaled. If the base point is inside or on the object,
the entity changes size at its present location. If the
base point is outside the object, the object moves from
its original location still in accordance with the scale
factor.

If you select the Scale factor option, specify a
relative scale factor. All selected entities are multiplied

by this factor. A factor of less than 1 shrinks the
entities; a factor of greater than 1 increases their size.

The Reference option enables you to reference the
length of an entity to indicate the new length. All other
selected entities change size according to the scale
generated by the reference.

Script

Runs script files within the Drawing Editor.

Syntax

```
Command: Script
Script file <default>:
```

Description

Use Script to run a script file from within the Drawing
Editor. To run the same script file again, use the
Rscript command.

Select

Creates a selection set for use in subsequent
commands.

Syntax

```
Command: Select
Select objects:
Select objects:
```

Description

After you use Select to create a selection set of entities,
you can use the selection set with subsequent
commands. You can use the Previous option with
an editing command to use the previously defined
selection set.

Setvar

Accesses system variables.

Syntax

```
Command: Setvar
Variable name or ?:
```

Description

The ? prompt enables you to list any system variable. Most of the uniquely named system variables can be called directly from the Command: prompt in Release 11. Should you want to modify a variable while executing a command, you can use Setvar transparently. In some cases, however, changes to the variable may not take effect until after the current command is completed. For more information on transparent commands, see the discussion of the apostrophe at the beginning of this Command Reference.

Sh

Provides access to the operating system.

Syntax

```
Command: Sh
DOS command:
```

Description

This command permits you to execute only one command at the system level, and then returns you to AutoCAD. The Sh command is similar to the Shell command, but loads a smaller version of your operating system.

Shade

Creates a limited shaded picture of the image in the current viewport.

Syntax

```
Command: Shade
```

Description

This command produces an image similar to AutoShade's "Quick Shade" option, based on the drawing's entities and the current view on-screen. This rendered image has limitations, however; only one light source is used. This source is located directly behind the viewer.

You cannot plot or select entities from this shaded image. You can save the image as a slide for later display, however, by using the Mslide command. To replace the original drawing, use Regen. Undo cannot remove the rendering from the screen.

Shape

Inserts shapes in the drawing.

Syntax

```
Command: Shape
Starting point:
Height <1.0>:
Rotation angle <0.0>:
```

Description

The `Starting point:` prompt asks for a location at which to insert the shape. This point corresponds to the first vector in the shape definition.

`Height <1.0>:` is used to scale the shape.

The shape can be rotated at a given angle, which you can specify at the `Rotation angle <0.0>:` prompt.

You must use the Load command to load shape files before you can use the shapes. Type **Load**, press Enter, and type the name of the file you want to load. You can use the question mark (?) to list available shape file names.

Shell

Provides full access to the operating system.

Syntax

```
Command: Shell
DOS command:
```

Description

At the DOS Command: prompt, you can execute an operating system command or press Enter to get to the system level. At the system level, you can execute as many commands as you want (even other programs). Return to AutoCAD by typing **Exit** at the operating system prompt.

If your system is based on UNIX, the prompt reads Shell Command:. The command you enter is passed to the Bourne shell by way of the *system* system function. The Shell command operates similarly in AutoCAD's other platforms. Consult the *AutoCAD Installation and Performance Guide* for more information.

Sketch

Permits freehand drawing.

Syntax

```
Command: Sketch
Record increment <current>:
Sketch. Pen eXit Quit Record Erase
Connect
```

Description

To select an option while you are in Sketch mode, all you need to do is type the capitalized letter. You do not need to press Enter. These options remain on-screen as you sketch.

AutoCAD sketches with line or polyline segments. Record increment is the length of these segments. Both Snap and Ortho modes affect the way segments are drawn.

The Pen option is a toggle that alternately raises and lowers the pen. If the pen is up, you can move the cursor on-screen without drawing. When the pen is down, AutoCAD draws as the cursor moves.

eXit records the segments permanently and ends Sketch mode.

Quit ends Sketch mode without saving any of the work.

Record saves the segments without exiting.

Erase erases segments as you backtrack through the drawing.

Connect joins new segments to existing segments. Make sure that the pen is up. Then position the cursor next to an existing segment and type C.

Sketch is not an option. It is merely a label indicating that you are working in Sketch mode.

Snap

Provides an invisible grid into which you lock.

Syntax

```
Command: Snap
Snap spacing or ON/OFF/Aspect/Rotate/
  Style <current>:
```

Description

Snap spacing is the default. Just like the Grid command, Snap spacing sets both the X and Y values. Simply type the values you want and press Enter. Values may be as large or as small as needed in the drawing.

Snap is a toggle. You can turn it on and off from within the command by selecting the ON and OFF options or by pressing F9.

Aspect sets the X and Y spacings to different values. You are prompted first for the X value and then for the Y value.

Select the `Rotate` option if you need to draw at an angle other than horizontal. You can rotate the grid and snap to accommodate the required angle. `Rotate` affects both the visible grid and the invisible snap mode. You are prompted for a base point, around which the grid is rotated. If you want to align the point with an entity, specify the entity for the rotation angle.

`Style` enables you to choose between standard drawing mode (the default) or isometric mode.

Snap mode can be toggled on and off from within commands as you work. You can toggle snap on and start to draw, and then toggle snap off while still in the command.

Solid

Draws solid rectilinear and triangular areas.

Syntax

```
Command: Solid
First point:
Second point:
Third point:
Fourth point:
Third point:
Fourth point:
```

Description

To draw a solid, indicate the area's corners. You must indicate the corners in the correct sequence to achieve the shape you want. You can indicate three or four corners.

To obtain a rectilinear solid, the points must be arranged so that the first and third points lie on the same edge. If you indicate the points in a clockwise or counterclockwise direction, you will get a bow-tie shape. If you are drawing only a four-point solid, press Enter when you are prompted the second time for the `Third point:`. If you are drawing a three-point solid, press Enter at the `Fourth point:` prompt. AutoCAD still prompts you to continue the command. If you continue, the solids are connected.

Status

Displays drawing information.

Syntax

```
Command: Status
```

Description

Status tells you how the toggles are set, what your drawing extents and limits are, how much disk space is available, and how much I/O page space is available.

You can issue this command from the Dim: prompt. When it is used in the dimensioning mode, Status displays a list of dimensioning variables, along with their current settings. If there are more variables than can fit on-screen at one time, press Enter to see the rest of the list.

Stretch

Changes entities while retaining connections with other entities or points.

Syntax

```
Command: Stretch
Select objects to stretch by
  window...
Select objects:
Base point:
New point:
```

Description

Use Stretch to "stretch" entities to make them smaller or larger, or to realign entities in any way you want. You must select the first object by a window (window or crossing). You can make subsequent selections by pointing. Another window selection negates the first window selection.

Style

Loads text fonts into the drawing.

Syntax

```
Command: Style
Text style name (or ?) <current>:
Font file <default>:
Height <default>:
Width factor <default>:
Oblique angle <default>:
Backwards? <Y/N>:
Upside-down? <Y/N>:
Vertical? <Y/N>:
(name) is now the current text style.
```

Description

In addition to enabling the loading of text fonts, this command is also available from the Dim: prompt. See the descriptions of Dim and Dim1 for information about dimensioning, as well as the Text and Dtext commands for uses of the Style subcommand.

Tablet

Enables you to turn the tablet on and off, calibrate the tablet for digitizing drawings, or configure the tablet for a menu.

Syntax

```
Command: Tablet
Option (ON/OFF/CAL/CFG):
```

Description

ON returns the tablet to menu use after it has been turned off. OFF turns off the tablet menu and enables you to use the entire tablet area for digitizing. Use the OFF option before calibrating.

CAL enables you to calibrate the tablet to a given paper drawing for the purpose of digitizing the paper drawing into AutoCAD. You are prompted for the following:

```
Digitize first known point:
Enter coordinates for first point:
Digitize second known point:
Enter coordinates for second point:
```

Secure the paper drawing to the digitizing tablet so that no movement can occur. On the drawing select two points that you know, and decide what coordinates those two points should have in AutoCAD. These are the first and second points, which define the drawing's scale.

CFG enables you to configure the tablet for different menu areas when you switch between menus. If the menus are defined with the same areas and the same number of squares in each area, you do not need to reconfigure the tablet. You are prompted for the following:

```
Enter number of tablet menus
   desired (0-4) <default>:
Digitize upper left corner of menu
   area n:
Digitize lower left corner of menu
   area n:
Digitize lower right corner of menu
   area n:
Digitize lower left corner of
   screen pointing area:
Digitize upper right corner of
   screen pointing area:
```

In these prompts, *n* represents the number of the tablet area you are defining. If you make a mistake while defining one of the corners, you must execute the command again. The screen pointing area that is specified includes the area used for the screen menu, which can be reached through the tablet or another pointing device.

Tabsurf

Creates a tabulated surface with a path and a direction vector.

Syntax

```
Command: Tabsurf
Select path curve:
Select direction vector:
```

Description

The `Select path curve:` prompt is used to define the surface. You can use lines, arcs, circles, and polylines.

The `Select direction vector:` prompt is a line or open polyline showing the direction and length of the surface.

Tedit

Controls the placement and orientation of associative dimension text.

Syntax

```
Dim: Tedit
Select dimension:
Enter text location (Left/Right/Home/
  Angle):
```

Description

AutoCAD drags the dimension text as you move the cursor. If you choose to modify a diameter, linear, or radius dimension, you can select `Left` or `Right`. These options justify the text along the dimension line.

The `Home` option places the text string at the default location. The string is given the default orientation as well. This option is the same as using the dimensioning subcommand Hometext.

If you select `Angle`, AutoCAD prompts:

```
Text angle:
```

To alter the angle, you can select two points or enter a number directly. The dimension text to be altered rotates around the center point.

This subcommand is used within the dimensioning
feature of AutoCAD. For more information, see the
Dim and Dim1 commands.

Text

Places text in a drawing.

Syntax

```
Command: Text
Justify/Style/<Start point>:
```

Description

Start point is the default for the Text command.
AutoCAD looks for the starting point for the text to be
inserted. The text is left-justified.

If you press Enter at this prompt, and text has been
entered before, AutoCAD prompts you for new text.
This text is placed below the last text entered and
retains all the parameters of the last text, including
font, height, rotation, and color.

If this is the first text string entered into the drawing
(or if you choose a point instead of pressing Enter), the
following prompt appears:

```
Height <current>:
Rotation angle <current>:
Text:
```

Press Enter after the text string to complete the
command.

After you initially enter the Text command, you can
align your text by selecting the Justify option. The
prompt that follows depends on the text's orientation.
If the text is horizontally oriented, AutoCAD prompts:

```
Align/Fit/Center/Middle/Right/TL/
    TC/TR/ML/MC/MR/BL/BC/BR:
```

If the text is vertically oriented, the following prompt
appears:

```
Align/Fit/Center/Middle/Right:
```

Align prompts for a start point and an ending point
for the text. The text is adjusted to print between the
two points.

Center centers the text. AutoCAD prompts for the
center point for the text.

Fit is similar to Align. AutoCAD prompts for the
text's starting and ending points, and for a height.
AutoCAD adjusts the text's width to fit between the
two points.

Middle is similar to Center. The difference is that
Middle centers text both horizontally and vertically
on the specified point. AutoCAD prompts for a middle
point.

Right right-justifies the text. You are prompted for
an endpoint for the text.

Select the TL (for Top-Left) option to specify the
upper left corner of the text string. The "top" of a text
string (as seen in TL, TC, and TR) depicts the highest
edge seen in the font's capital letters. Select TC (for
Top-Center) to insert the string so that it is centered on
the upper edge of the capital letters. To insert text so
that it is right-justified with the selected location being
the upper edge of the capital letters, use TR (for Top-
Right).

Select ML (for Middle-Left) if you want the selected
point to be the left edge of the string and the text's
height to be centered. MC (for Middle-Center) centers
the text both horizontally and vertically on the selected
point. This option is the same as the Middle option,
mentioned previously. Use MR (for Middle-Right) to
make the text string right-justified and centered
vertically.

BL (for Bottom-Left) left-justifies the text based on the
string's lowest point, typically the descender of
lowercase letters, such as the "hook" of a lowercase
g or *j*. To insert the string centered on the lowest point
of the line of text, choose BC (for Bottom-Center). The
last option, BR (for Bottom-Right), right-justifies the
text and uses the lowest point of the line as its insertion
point.

After you respond with one of the preceding options, AutoCAD displays the following prompts:

```
Height <current>:
Rotation angle <current>:
Text:
```

If you press Enter at this prompt, AutoCAD prompts you for text. This new text is placed below the last text entered and retains all the parameters of the last text, including font, height, rotation, and color.

After you respond to the preceding prompts, AutoCAD either prompts for the endpoints of the base line, or displays the following prompts:

```
Height <current>:
Rotation <current>:
Text:
```

You can include spaces in the text. When you finish typing the text, press Enter.

The default text font (called STANDARD) is used unless other fonts have been loaded with the Style command. You can insert some special characters with your text, but they are embedded within the text and must be activated by special codes. The following table shows these codes and the special characters they activate:

Code	Character
%%o	Overscore
%%u	Underscore
%%d	Degrees symbol
%%p	Plus/minus symbol
%%c	Circle diameter
%%%	Percent sign
%%nnn	ASCII character code *nnn*

After you place text strings in a drawing, you can alter the text by using the Ddedit or Change commands.

The third and final option of the original Text prompt is the Style option. By selecting Style, you can switch between the defined styles and loaded text fonts. See Style for procedures on loading text fonts.

Textscr

Flips to the text screen on a single-screen system.

Syntax

    Command: **Textscr**

Description

Textscr is the opposite of the Graphscr command; this command switches the screen from graphics mode to text mode. You also can switch between graphics and text modes by pressing F1.

Textscr can be used transparently. For more information about transparent commands, see the discussion of the apostrophe at the beginning of this Command Reference.

Time

Keeps track of time spent in a drawing.

Syntax

    Command: **Time**

Description

When you enter this command, AutoCAD responds with a display similar to the following (with values displayed to the right of each item):

    Current time:
    Drawing created:
    Drawing last updated:
    Time in drawing editor:
    Elapsed timer:
    Timer on.

    Display/ON/OFF/Reset:

Display redisplays the time. ON turns on the timer; OFF turns it off. The Reset option resets the timer to 0.

`Drawing created:` is the date and time of the current drawing's creation.

`Drawing last updated:` is the last time you saved the current file.

`Time in drawing editor:` is the total time spent in all the Drawing Editor sessions with this drawing.

`Elapsed timer:` shows the time spent in the Drawing Editor during the current session.

Trace

Draws a line of a specific width.

Syntax

```
Command: Trace
Trace width:
From point:
To point:
To point:
```

Description

Trace is a seldom-used AutoCAD command that draws lines with widths. Polylines are more commonly used because they are far easier to edit.

Trim

Trims entities back to a boundary.

Syntax

```
Command: Trim
Select cutting edge(s):
Select object:
```

Description

The cutting edges are the boundaries to which you are trimming. After you specify all boundaries, AutoCAD prompts:

```
<Select object to trim>/Undo:
```

The Undo option enables you to restore the previously
trimmed entity to its original length.

Trotate

Enables the rotation of associative dimension text
strings.

Syntax

```
Dim: Trotate
Enter new text angle:
Select objects:
```

Description

When selecting the new angle, you can choose two
points or enter a value directly. If you choose an angle
of 0, AutoCAD positions the text string at the default
rotation.

As with other dimensioning subcommands, Trotate
must be used at the Dim: prompt. For more
information on AutoCAD's dimensioning feature and
commands, see Dim and Dim1.

U

Reverses the effect of the most recent command.

Syntax

```
Command: U
```

Description

This command is similar to Undo, but only reverses the
preceding command. Undo can optionally reverse a
group of previous commands.

Ucs

Defines or modifies User Coordinate Systems.

Syntax

```
Command: Ucs
Origin/ZAxis/3point/Entity/View/X/Y/
    Z/Prev/Restor/Save/Del/?/<World>:
```

Description

Origin defines a new UCS by moving the origin of the current UCS. The axis' orientation remains the same.

ZAxis defines a new UCS using an origin and a point indicating the positive Z axis. You are prompted:

```
Origin point <0,0,0>:
Point on positive portion of the
    z axis <default>:
```

3point defines a new UCS with three points: origin, positive X axis, and positive Y axis. You can use object snap modes to indicate a UCS that corresponds to entities in the drawing. You are prompted:

```
Origin point <0,0,0>:
Point on the positive portion of
    the X axis <current>:
Point on positive-Y portion of the
    UCS X-Y plane <current>:
```

The three points must not form a straight line.

Entity defines a new UCS using an existing entity. The X-Y plane is parallel to the X-Y plane that was in effect when the entity was drawn, and has the same Z direction as that of the indicated entity. The entity must be indicated by pointing. The following list describes the process of creating the UCS from each type of entity:

Arc–The center becomes the origin; the X axis passes through the point on the arc closest to the pick point.

Circle–Same as Arc.

Dimension–The insertion point is the origin; the X axis is parallel to the UCS of the dimension.

Line–The endpoint nearest the pick point is the new origin; the Y axis is the other end of the line segment indicated.

Point–The origin is the point; the X axis is derived arbitrarily.

Polyline–The start point is the new origin; the X axis lies from the origin to the next vertex.

Mesh–The start point is the new origin; the X axis lies from the origin to the next vertex.

Solid–The first point of solid is the origin; the X axis is on the line between the first and second points.

Trace–The first points are the origin; the X axis lies along the center of the trace.

3D Face–The first points are the origin; the X axis is defined by the first two points; and the positive Y side is from the first and fourth points.

Shape–The origin is the insertion point; the X axis is defined by the rotation.

Text–The origin is the insertion point; the X axis is defined by the rotation.

Block–The origin is the insertion point; the X axis is defined by the rotation.

View defines a new UCS whose Z axis is parallel to the direction of view—that is, perpendicular to the current view.

X/Y/Z rotates the current UCS around the specified axis. You are prompted for the rotation around the axis.

Previous takes you back to the UCS in which you last worked.

Restore restores a saved UCS.

Save saves the current UCS. You must supply a file name that adheres to your operating system's conventions.

Delete removes the specified UCS from the list. You
are prompted for the name of the UCS to delete.

? lists the UCSs that are saved.

World sets the current coordinate system to the World
Coordinate System.

Ucsicon

Controls the User Coordinate System icon that appears
at the bottom of the drawing.

Syntax

Command: **Ucsicon**
All/Noorigin/ORigin <current>:

Description

All activates the icon change in all viewports, not just
the current port.

Noorigin (the default) displays the icon at all times
in the screen's lower left corner.

ORigin displays the icon at the origin of the
current UCS.

OFF turns off the icon; ON turns on the icon.

Undefine

Enables advanced programmers to assign new
definitions to standard AutoCAD commands.

Syntax

Command: **Undefine**
Command name:

Description

The indicated command is defined to the LISP routine
currently bearing the command name.

Undo

Reverses the effect of previous commands and provides control over the Undo feature.

Syntax

Command: **Undo**
Auto/Back/Control/End/Group/Mark/
    <Number>:

Description

Number is the default. You can enter the number of commands you want undone at this time. If you are stepping back to a particular point in the drawing, you can undo a specific number of commands at a time.

Auto prompts ON/OFF. This is the part of Undo that controls how menu selections and other multiple commands are handled. If Auto is on, the menu selections are treated as one command.

Group starts the grouping process. If you start the grouping process, you must end that process. When commands are grouped together, they are undone with one Undo command.

Use Mark to place a marker in your undo information; you then can return to the marker by using the Back option. You can mark more than one place at a time. When you go back to that mark, the mark is removed.

Back takes you back to the mark you placed in the undo information. If there are no marks in the undo information, AutoCAD undoes to the beginning of the editing session.

Control enables you to limit the Undo and U commands. AutoCAD prompts:

    All/None/One:

All is the default, and gives you access to all Undo functions. None disables the Undo command, and One permits one undo at a time. Both None and One free any disk space used for storing previous Undos.

You also can issue Undo from the Dim: prompt. If used while in dimensioning mode, Undo undoes the

last dimension inserted in the drawing. See the
descriptions of the Dim and Dim1 commands for
information on dimensioning.

Units

Sets the display format and precision of drawing units.

Syntax

Command: **Units**

Description

When you issue this command, AutoCAD displays a
prompt requesting the system units to be used.

The precision of the angle measurement is selected
next.

Next, you are prompted for the direction of angle 0.
The default in AutoCAD is for angle 0 to be at
"3 o'clock" and for all other angles to be figured
counterclockwise from 0.

The Units prompt controls the direction of angles. By
default, AutoCAD works counterclockwise. You can
work clockwise or counterclockwise.

Update

Updates associative dimensions to current dimension
variables.

Syntax

Dim: **Update**
Select objects:

Description

This dimensioning subcommand is available only from
the Dim: prompt. See the descriptions of the Dim and
Dim1 commands for information about dimensioning.

Variables

Lists the variable settings of a particular dimension style.

Syntax

```
Dim: Variables
Current dimension style:
?/Enter dimension style name or
  RETURN to select dimension:
Select dimension:
```

Description

If you provide the name of a dimension style, AutoCAD presents a list of the dimensioning variables and their values for that style. The question mark (?) presents a list of currently named dimension styles.

Vertical

Inserts a vertical (Y) dimension.

Syntax

```
Dim: Vertical
First extension line origin or Return
  to select:
Second extension line origin:
Dimension line location:
Dimension text <value>:
```

Description

This dimensioning subcommand is available only from the Dim: prompt. See the descriptions of the Dim and Dim1 commands for information about dimensioning.

View

Creates views of zoomed work areas.

Syntax

```
Command:  View
?/Delete/Restore/Save/Window:
View name:
```

Description

The ? option lists all the views that currently exist in the drawing. AutoCAD lists each view and designates each view with an M or a P to indicate whether the view was defined in model or paper space.

Delete removes the defined view from the list of saved views. This feature accepts wild cards or multiple views separated by commas.

Restore causes the view to be restored to the screen after it has been defined. Use Restore to flip between the views.

Save saves whatever is currently on-screen as a view. You are prompted for a view name, which can be 31 characters long and may contain letters, numbers, dollar signs ($), hyphens (-), and underscores (_). You reference the view by its view name.

Window lets you make several views without zooming in on a view. You put a window around the area you want to be in the view.

View can be used transparently. For more information on transparent commands, see the discussion of the apostrophe at the beginning of this Command Reference. A transparent View command cannot be used when a Vpoint, Dview, Zoom, Pan, or another View command is active. Further, View cannot be used transparently while you are working in paper space or if the display needs to be regenerated.

Viewports or Vports

Controls the number of viewports on-screen.

Syntax

```
Command:  Vports
Save/Restore/Delete/Join/Off/?/2/
  <3>/4:
```

Description

Save saves the current viewport configuration for future use. You are not limited to the number of viewports that can be saved. You are prompted for the name of the viewports; standard requirements apply to the name.

Restore restores a saved viewport.

Delete deletes a saved viewport configuration.

Join merges two adjacent viewports into one large view. The resulting viewport's size is obtained from the dominant viewport and the merged viewport. The image displayed is the one shown in the dominant viewport. You are prompted:

```
Select dominant viewport <current>:
Select viewport to merge:
```

Off returns you to single-viewport (normal) viewing.

The ? option lists the viewports that are currently saved.

The 2, 3, and 4 options enable you to define 2, 3, or 4 viewports in a configuration of your choice. Two viewports are defined with either a vertical or horizontal configuration. Three viewports are defined with one large port next to two small ports. Four viewports divide the screen into four equal areas.

Viewres

Controls AutoCAD's fast regeneration and the resolution of circles and arcs as they are drawn and represented.

Syntax

```
Command: Viewres
Do you want fast zooms? <Y>:
Enter circle zoom percent <1-20000)
  <100>:
```

Description

If you respond **Y** to the first prompt, AutoCAD enables fast regenerations. The circle zoom percent is the value that determines the resolution of circles and arcs in AutoCAD. The default is 100. The Viewres can be set from a resolution of 1 (lowest) to 20,000 (highest).

Vplayer

Controls a layer's visibility within individual viewports.

Syntax

```
Command: Vplayer
?/Freeze/Thaw/Reset/Newfrz/Vpvisdflt:
```

Description

Before adjusting the layer's aspects for individual viewports, you must use the Layer command to turn on and thaw the layer globally. After you select one of the Vplayer command's options, AutoCAD prompts you for the viewport to be affected, as follows:

```
All/Select/<Current>:
```

All instructs AutoCAD to make the alterations to every viewport defined in the drawing. This includes any viewport, visible or not.

The Select option prompts you to Select objects: and waits until you choose one or more viewports. Any changes to a layer's visibility is made only in the selected viewports.

If you press **C** (for current) or press Enter in reponse to the prompt, AutoCAD modifies only the current viewport.

The main Vplayer prompt is

```
?/Freeze/Thaw/Reset/Newfrz/
  Vpvisdflt:
```

From this you can obtain a listing of the layers currently frozen by selecting ?. AutoCAD prompts

`Select a viewport`: first; then you receive a listing of the layers currently frozen in that viewport.

Choosing the `Freeze` option instructs AutoCAD to freeze one or more layers in a viewport. You also can choose more than one viewport to affect. The following prompts appear:

```
Layer(s) to Freeze:
All/Select/<Current>:
```

The `Thaw` option makes visible layers in a given viewport and works in similar fashion to the `Freeze` option.

Use `Reset` to restore the default settings for the specified viewport. The viewport's default settings are established by the `Vpvisdft` option, which is discussed later. AutoCAD displays the following prompt:

```
Layer(s) to Reset:
All/Select/<Current>:
```

The `Newfrz` option creates one or more a new layers, which are frozen in all viewports. Use this feature if you want a new layer specifically for a viewport. The `Newfrz` prompt is

```
New viewport frozen layer name(s):
```

After creating the new layer, use the Thaw command to thaw the layer in that viewport. To specify multiple layers, separate the names with commas.

To better manage views as they are created, AutoCAD offers the `Vpvisdft` option, which establishes each layer's default visibility in newly created viewports. When you select this option, AutoCAD displays the following prompts:

```
Layer name(s) to change default
  viewport visibility:
Change default viewport visibility
  to Frozen/<Thawed>:
```

As with most of AutoCAD's layer prompts, you can enter wild-card names, as well as multiple names separated by commas.

Vpoint

Enables you to see a drawing from any point in model space.

Syntax

```
Command: Vpoint
Rotate/<View point><current>:
```

Description

The default view point is 0,0,1. When you want to return to the plan view of your drawing, type those coordinates at the prompt. You also can use the pull-down menus to determine your view point.

Vslide

Enables you to view previously created slides.

Syntax

```
Command: Vslide
Slide file <default>:
```

Description

Vslide (for View Slide) works with Mslide. You can view slides individually or in groups. A group of slides is called a *library*. To view slides from a slide library, respond as follows:

```
Command: Vslide
Slide file: library(slide)
```

Wblock

Writes drawing blocks out to individual drawing files, enabling blocks created in one drawing to be used in several drawings.

Syntax

```
Command: Wblock
File name:
Block name:
```

Description

At the `File name` prompt, specify the name of the file you are creating to hold the block. The file name must comply with your operating system's file-naming conventions.

At the `Block name` prompt, tell AutoCAD which block you want to write to the file. If the block does not yet exist, press Enter; AutoCAD then displays the standard block-creation prompts. If the block and the file have the same name, you can type the equal sign (=) shorthand character. If the entire drawing is being written out, use the asterisk (*). Otherwise, type the name of the block to be written to the file.

Files created with Wblock are normal drawing files that can be edited and viewed in much the same way as other drawing files. Entities written out with Wblock are placed in model space of the new file unless the * option is used. Entities then are placed in whichever space they occupy in the current drawing.

Xbind

Enables you to add specific pieces of an externally referenced file into the current drawing permanently.

Syntax

```
Command: Xbind
Block/Dimstyle/LAyer/LType/Style:
```

Description

Each Xbind option enables you to specify the entities you want to add into your drawing file. For example, `LAyer` lets you add layers from an externally referenced file into the current drawing.

Xref

Enables you to use and display an externally
referenced file within your drawing.

Syntax

```
Command: Xref
?/Bind/Detach/Path/Reload/<Attach>:
```

Description

The ? option lists all the externally referenced files in
use within the current drawing.

Bind enables you to attach an externally referenced
file into the current drawing permanently. This file is
then referenced internally as a typical block entity.
Detach removes all references to an externally
referenced file from the current drawing. This is the
same as using the Purge command to remove a block
from the drawing.

Path enables you to redefine the path used to locate
an externally referenced file. These files, like any other
files created by your operating system, can be moved.
In order to use the file with Xref, the path must
accurately point to the file's location.

Reload enables you to update an externally
referenced file used within the current drawing at any
time.

Attach inserts the externally referenced file into the
current drawing.

Zoom

Enables you to magnify the image.

Syntax

```
Command: Zoom
All/Center/Dynamic/Extents/Left/
  Previous/Vmax/Window/<Scale(X/XP)>:
```

Description

All returns you to your drawing limits or to the extents, whichever is larger.

Center enables you to identify a new center point for the screen and then to enter the height. This height is the factor that determines the zoom scale.

Dynamic causes a new screen to appear on the monitor.

The drawing's extents contain the precise area in which you have drawn. The X and Y values make up the drawing extents. The Extents option, therefore, pulls all entities in the drawing onto the screen. This is a good way to see whether any "rogue entities" are floating around in the drawing.

Left enables you to set a new lower left corner and height.

Previous returns you to the previous screen.

The Vmax option enables you to zoom "out" as far as possible without forcing a regeneration. The image generated is redrawn at redraw speed. Because of speed improvements, the Vmax option may often be preferred over the All option, which often forces a regeneration.

Window enables you to place a window around the area in which you want to work.

Scale enables you to zoom by a scale factor. If you follow this factor with an X, the new view is developed relative to the current view. Hence, entering 2X creates a view showing the object twice as large as the previous view. The XP option enables you to develop an image whose size is scaled relative to the paper space. As such, you can establish many details of a variety of scales for the same object.

Like many other commands, Zoom can be used transparently. You cannot use a transparent Zoom command, however, if it would force a screen regeneration, if you are working in paper space, or while a Vpoint, Dview, Zoom, Pan, or View command is active. For more information on transparent commands, see the discussion of the apostrophe at the beginning of this Command Reference.

3Dface

Draws three-dimensional flat planes.

Syntax

```
Command: 3Dface
First point:
Second point:
Third point:
Fourth point:
Third point:
Fourth point:
```

Description

3Dface drawings are similar to the Solid drawings created in the X-Y plane. The prompt sequence is similar to that of the Solid command. The difference is in the point input; the points used to define the 3Dface continue around the edge, either clockwise or counterclockwise. If you want to make one or more edges of the 3Dface invisible, enter an I before selecting the beginning point of that edge.

3Dmesh

Enables you to create a general polygon mesh by specifying the mesh's size (in terms of M and N) and vertexes.

Syntax

```
Command: 3Dmesh
Mesh M size:
Mesh N size:
Vertex (0,0):
Vertex (x,y):
Vertex (x,y):
Vertex (x,y):
```

Description

M size and N size define how many vertexes the mesh will have (M x N).

Select Vertex to specify the mesh's vertexes. Default vertexes correspond to the current UCS and to the M and N sizes. Vertexes may be two- or three-dimensional points.

The 3Dmesh command, which is used for specifying arbitrary meshes, is best used in LISP. For easier uses of meshes, see Rulesurf, Tabsurf, Revsurf, and Edgesurf.

3Dpoly

Draws three-dimensional polylines.

Syntax

```
Command: 3Dpoly
From point:
Close/Undo/<Endpoint of line>:
```

Description

At the From point: prompt, specify the polyline's starting point.

Select the Close option to close a polyline with two or more segments.

Undo undoes the last end point.

The Endpoint of line prompt asks for the polyline's next endpoint.

Points can be two- or three-dimensional. Use the Pedit command to edit three-dimensional polylines.

SYSTEM VARIABLES

This is a complete listing of all AutoCAD system variables, including those affecting dimensioning. Each variable generally has a default value, which is saved with the drawing or another AutoCAD file. AutoCAD makes use of the following types of variables:

- Integer
- Real
- Text String
- Two-Dimensional Point
- Three-Dimensional Point
- Toggles (On and Off)

Many AutoCAD system variables are *read-only* (that is, they cannot be changed directly) because they are used internally by different AutoCAD commands. You can use the Setvar command to change any variables that are not read-only. With Release 11, however, many system variables may be changed directly at the `Command:` prompt, which eliminates any need to use the Setvar command first.

Unless otherwise noted, all these system variables' values are saved with the AutoCAD drawing.

ACADPREFIX

If you specified a directory other than the AutoCAD directory for your drawing, that directory's name is stored here. This string variable is read-only.

ACADVER

The current release of AutoCAD. If you are using Release 11, the default should be 11. This string variable is read-only.

AFLAGS

Contains information that determines whether attributes are

1	invisible
2	constant
3	verify
4	preset

This integer variable defaults to 0 and is set when the Attdef command is first executed.

ANGBASE

This real-number variable calculates all angles in AutoCAD. It contains the direction for angle 0, which is set to a default of 3 o'clock.

ANGDIR

This integer variable determines whether angles default to clockwise (0) or counterclockwise (1). Counterclockwise is the default.

APERTURE

APERTURE defines object snap target (aperture) height. This integer variable defaults to 10 and is set with the Aperture command. It is saved in the ACAD.CFG configuration file.

AREA

This real-number variable holds the value of the true area from the most recent of any of the following commands: Area, List, or Dblist. AREA is read-only and defaults to 0.

ATTDIA

This integer variable's value determines whether the Insert command displays a dialogue box for any attributes defined with a given block. A value of 1 displays a dialogue box; 0 (the default) does not.

ATTMODE

This integer variable holds the value of the Attdisp command. A value of 0 turns attribute display off; 1 (the default) indicates normal display; 2 turns the display on.

ATTREQ

This variable's value controls the treatment of attributes as they are inserted. If ATTREQ's value is 0, all attributes are set to their default values upon insertion. If ATTREQ's value is 1, AutoCAD prompts you for attributes. This integer variable defaults to a value of 1.

AUNITS

This integer variable holds the angular units set with the Units command. Those units are assigned the following values:

0	decimal degrees
1	degrees/minutes/seconds
2	grads
3	radians
4	surveyor's units

The default value is 0.

AUPREC

This variable's value is an integer that indicates the precision of angular units. AUPREC's value defaults to 0.

AXISMODE

This integer variable controls axis display (Axis command). A value of 0 (the default) turns off axis display; a value of 1 turns on axis display.

AXISUNIT

This two-dimensional point dictates the spacing of tick marks for the Axis command. AXISUNIT's value defaults to 0,0. A change to this variable is not reflected in the displayed grid and axis until the screen's contents are redrawn.

BACKZ

The value of BACKZ is the offset for the back clipping plane, and is set with the Dview command. The units are drawing units. You can find the distance from the target to the clipping plane by using the following formula: Camera-to-target minus BACKZ equals distance. This real number variable is read-only.

BLIPMODE

BLIPMODE is a toggle that controls whether blips appear on-screen. Use the Blipmode command to set BLIPMODE's value. A value of 1 turns on blips.

CDATE

This real-number variable holds the current date and time for the drawing. CDATE is read-only.

CECOLOR

This variable holds the color with which you are currently drawing. The default value is BYLAYER, which means that the color defaults to the current layer color. CECOLOR is a read-only string variable.

CELTYPE

CELTYPE holds the linetype with which you are currently drawing. The default value is BYLAYER, which means that the linetype defaults to the current layer linetype. CELTYPE is a read-only string variable.

CHAMFERA

The value of CHAMFERA is a real number that holds the first chamfer distance. The default value is 0.

CHAMFERB

Like CHAMFERA, CHAMFERB is a real number. CHAMFERB's value is the second chamfer distance. The default value is 0.

CLAYER

This read-only text string holds the current layer's name.

CMDECHO

CMDECHO determines whether commands are echoed to the screen as you enter them. This integer variable is used for programming purposes. The default value is 1.

COORDS

This integer variable controls coordinate display at the top of the screen. If COORDS is set to 0 (the default value), the coordinate display is updated only when you pick a point; if the variable's value is 1, the coordinate display is updated as the crosshairs travel around the screen.

CVPORT

This integer variable holds the identification for the current viewport. The default value is 4.

DATE

This real-number variable holds the current Julian calendar date and time. DATE is read-only.

DIMALT

DIMALT is a toggle that controls the generation of alternative dimensions. The default value is 0 (Off).

DIMALTD

This integer value controls the decimal places for alternative dimension value. DIMALTD defaults to a value of 2.

DIMALTF

AutoCAD multiplies this real-number value (the alternative units scale factor) with the value determined by the current dimension. If DIMALT is on, the alternative value appears along with the normal value.

This variable defaults to 25.4 (for displaying alternative distances in millimeters).

DIMAPOST

This text-string variable holds the suffix for alternative dimensions. DIMAPOST is read-only at the `Command:` prompt; it can be set only at the `Dim:` prompt.

DIMASO

DIMASO is a toggle that controls the generation of associative dimensions. If set to a value of 1 (the default), dimensions are associative; if DIMASO is 0, dimensions are normal.

DIMASZ

This real number indicates the dimensioning arrow size. AutoCAD uses this size, the size of the text, and a default minimum length for the dimension line to determine whether dimension text will be inside or outside the dimension. The default value is 0.18.

DIMBLK

If you need an indicator other than arrows or tick marks at the end of dimension strings, you can create a block and indicate its name here. This string variable is read-only at the `Command:` prompt; it can be set only at the `Dim:` prompt.

DIMBLK1

If you want one arrow on the dimension line to be different from the other arrow, DIMBLK1 is placed on the end of the dimension line that extends to the first extension line. This string variable is read-only at the `Command:` prompt; it can be set only at the `Dim:` prompt.

DIMBLK2

If you want one arrow on the dimension line to be different from the other, DIMBLK2 is placed on the end of the dimension line that extends to the second extension line. This string variable is read-only at the `Command:` prompt; it can be set only at the `Dim:` prompt.

DIMCEN

DIMCEN is a real-number variable that determines the size of the center mark that AutoCAD inserts with

the Center command. The default is 0.09. The size
is the distance from the center mark along one of the line
segments.

DIMDLE2

If you are using tick marks, this real-number variable
can be used to extend the dimension line past the
extension lines. DIMDLE2 defaults to 0.

DIMCLRD

This integer determines which color AutoCAD uses
when drawing dimension lines. The color number is the
same as that used by the Layer or Color command.

DIMCLRE

This integer determines which color AutoCAD uses
when drawing dimension extension lines. The color
number is the same as that used by the Layer or Color
command.

DIMCLRT

DIMCLRT determines which color AutoCAD uses
when drawing dimension text. The color number is the
same as that used by the Layer or Color command.

DIMDLI

DIMDLI is a real-number variable that controls the
increment size AutoCAD uses to offset dimensions
(default is 0.38) when using the Baseline and Continue
dimension commands.

DIMEXE

DIMEXE controls the length of extension lines above
the dimension line. If you do not want the extension line
to extend beyond the dimension line, change this real-
number variable from the default of 0.18 to 0.

DIMEXO

DIMEXO controls the offset of an extension line from
the origin. If you do not want an offset, set this real-
number variable from the default of 0.0625 to 0.

DIMGAP

This real-number variable determines the space between
dimension text and dimension lines when a dimension
line is broken to accommodate text.

DIMLFAC

DIMLFAC sets the drawing's scale factor. The default value (1) sets the drawing to full scale (one drawing inch equals one object inch). If you are drawing in one-half scale, set this variable to 2. AutoCAD multiplies the measured values by this real-number variable. Angular dimensions are not affected.

DIMLIM

DIMLIM is a toggle that controls whether limits are generated using the values in DIMTM and DIMTP. The default is off (0).

DIMPOST

This string variable holds a default suffix for dimension text. You can enter a suffix to be attached to dimensions as they are inserted. This variable is read-only at the `Command:` prompt; it can be set only at the `Dim:` prompt.

DIMSAH

DIMSAH is a toggle; if it is on (with a value of 1), AutoCAD uses block names in DIMBLK1 and DIMBLK2 as arrowheads for dimensioning. The default value, 0, turns DIMSAH off.

DIMSCALE

DIMSCALE is a real-number variable that scales an entire dimension by its value. This variable is useful when you are working with either a large or an extremely small drawing. To invoke paper-space scaling, set DIMSCALE to 0. This variable defaults to 1.

DIMSE1

This variable is a toggle that controls suppression of the first extension line. DIMSE1 defaults to a value of 0, which turns off suppression.

DIMSE2

This variable is a toggle that controls suppression of the second extension line. DIMSE2 defaults to a value of 0, which turns off suppression.

DIMSHO

When this toggle is on (that is, when its value is 1), dimension values are updated as a dimension changes.

When DIMSHO is set to the default value of 0, dimension text is updated after the change.

DIMSOXD

This toggle suppresses outside-extension dimension lines. DIMSOXD defaults to a value of 0, which turns off suppression.

DIMTAD

This toggle controls placement of dimension text above a dimension line. DIMTAD defaults to a value of 0 (Off), meaning that the dimension line is broken in order to place the dimension text within it.

DIMTIH

DIMTIH draws all text horizontally inside the dimensions (parallel to bottom edge of the paper). When this toggle is turned off, text is aligned with the dimension line and is readable from the bottom or right side of drawing. The default is on (1).

DIMTIX

This toggle forces dimension text to appear between extension lines, even if dimension lines and arrows do not fit. DIMTIX defaults to a value of 0 (Off).

DIMTM

DIMTM is a real number that sets negative tolerances for dimensions. The default value is 0.

DIMTOFL

This toggle forces AutoCAD to draw dimension lines between extension lines, even if the dimension text is forced outside. The default value is 0 (Off).

DIMTOH

DIMTOH draws all text horizontally outside the dimensions. When this toggle is turned off (that is, set to a value of 0), dimension text is aligned with dimension lines and is readable from the bottom or right side of the page. The default value, 1, turns the toggle on.

DIMTOL

DIMTOL is a toggle that causes tolerance generation using tolerance settings defined in DIMTP and DIMTM. The default value, 0, turns the toggle off.

DIMTP

This real-number variable (the default value is 0) defines positive tolerances for dimensions.

DIMTSZ

This real-number variable (the default value is 0) sets a size for tick marks. If you want arrowheads, specify 0 for tick mark size.

DIMTVP

DIMTVP enables you to place dimension text above or below a dimension line. AutoCAD uses the calculation DIMTVP x DIMTXT to place the text. To use this variable, DIMTAD must be off. If the real-number value of DIMTVP is positive, text is placed above the dimension line; if negative, text is placed below the dimension line. This variable defaults to 0.

DIMTXT

DIMTXT is a real number that controls text size for dimensions. The default value is 0.18.

DIMZIN

DIMZIN is an integer variable that controls AutoCAD's zero-inch editing feature of dimensioning when you are working with architectural units. If the variable is set to 0 (the default value), zero feet and zero inches are not placed in dimensions. If 1, both zero feet and zero inches are placed in dimensions. If 2, only zero feet is placed in dimensions; if 3, only zero inches is placed in dimensions.

DISTANCE

This real-number variable indicates the last value computed by the Dist command. DISTANCE is read-only.

DRAGMODE

DRAGMODE is an integer variable that controls the dragging of entities. The default setting of 2 means that AutoCAD displays a ghosted image of the entities selected as they are being dragged.

DRAGP1

DRAGP1 controls the speed at which entities being Regen-dragged are redrawn. The default value is 10.

This integer variable is saved in the ACAD.CFG configuration file.

DRAGP2

DRAGP2 controls the speed at which entities being Fast-dragged are redrawn. The default value is 25. This integer variable is saved in the ACAD.CFG configuration file.

DWGNAME

This string variable contains the name of current drawing. DWGNAME is read-only.

DWGPREFIX

This string variable contains the path for the current drawing. DWGPREFIX is read-only.

ELEVATION

ELEVATION is a real number representing the value for the current elevation relative to the current UCS.

ERRNO

This integer variable holds error codes caused by AutoLISP and ADS applications. ERRNO is not saved.

EXPERT

This integer variable controls the issuance of Are you sure? prompts, as follows:

Value	Prompts suppressed
0	(Default) Issues all prompts normally.
1	Suppresses About to regen, proceed? and Do you really want to turn the current layer off? prompts.
2	Suppresses the preceding prompts, the Block already defined. Redefine it? and A drawing with this name already exists. Overwrite it? prompts.
3	Suppresses the preceding prompts and those issued by the Linetype command if you try to load a linetype that is already loaded, or to create a new linetype in a file that already defines it.

4 Suppresses the preceding prompts, and those issued by Ucs Save and Vports Save commands if the name you supply already exists.

5 Suppresses all preceding prompts, as well as new prompts issued by the Dim Save and Dim Override commands, if the style name already exists.

When a prompt is suppressed by EXPERT, the operation is performed as though you respond **Y** to the prompt.

EXTMAX

EXTMAX is a three-dimensional (X,Y,Z) point indicating the upper right coordinate of the area in which you have drawn. This variable is read-only.

EXTMIN

EXTMIN is a three-dimensional (X,Y,Z) point indicating the lower left coordinate of the area in which you have drawn. This variable is read-only.

FILEDIA

This integer variable, when set to a value of 1, presents a dialogue box when requesting file information. When FILEDIA is set to 0, AutoCAD requests file information at the `Command:` prompt.

FILLETRAD

This real-number variable (the default value is 0) indicates the radius used by the Fillet command.

FILLMODE

This integer determines whether polylines and solids are filled with color. The default value is 1.

FRONTZ

FRONTZ stores the location of the front clipping plane as defined with the Dview command. The location of the front clipping plane can be found by subtracting FRONTZ from the camera-to-target distance. This real-number variable defaults to 0, and is read-only.

GRIDMODE

GRIDMODE is an integer variable that turns the grid on and off. The default value is 0 (Off).

GRIDUNIT

GRIDUNIT is a two-dimensional variable that sets grid spacing for the current viewport. This variable defaults to 0,0. A change to this variable is not reflected in the displayed grid and axis until the screen is redrawn.

HANDLES

The HANDLES toggle is used to turn entity handles on or off. This read-only variable's default value is 0.

HIGHLIGHT

This integer (the default is 1) controls whether entities selected for a particular operation are highlighted.

INSBASE

INSBASE is a three-dimensional point indicating the drawing's insertion base point. The default is 0,0,0 in the WCS.

LASTANGLE

This real-number variable represents the end angle of the last arc entered, relative to the X-Y plane of the current UCS or current space. LASTANGLE is read-only.

LASTPOINT

LASTPOINT is a three-dimensional point with a default setting of 0,0,0. The variable indicates the last point entered, in UCS coordinates for the current space.

LENSLENGTH

LENSLENGTH determines the length of the AutoCAD lens, in millimeters (default 50). Used in perspective viewing, this real-number variable is set with the Dview command. LENSLENGTH is read-only.

LIMCHECK

This integer variable controls the limits-check alarm. LIMCHECK defaults to 0.

LIMMAX

LIMMAX is a two-dimensional point representing the upper right drawing limits, in World coordinates relative to the current space.

LIMMIN

LIMMIN is a two-dimensional point (default 0,0) representing the lower left drawing limits in World coordinates relative to the current space.

LTSCALE

This real-number variable indicates the global linetype scale factor. The default value is 1.

LUNITS

This integer holds the value set for units with the Units command. The default value is 2.

LUPREC

This integer determines the number of decimal places for linear units. The default value is 4.

MAXACTVP

This integer variable holds the number of viewports that AutoCAD can regenerate at one time.

MAXSORT

This integer number tells AutoCAD how many files or named objects (layers, blocks, and so forth) can be sorted and displayed in alphanumeric order. The default value is 200.

MENUECHO

MENUECHO is an integer that controls menu echo and prompting. This value represents the sum of the following (note that digits at left are binary based):

0   (Default) Displays all menu items and system prompts
1   Suppresses echo of menu items
2   Suppresses printing of system prompts
4   Disables ^P toggle of menu-item echoing

MENUNAME

MENUNAME is a string that holds the name of the menu file currently in use. This variable is read-only but can be set with the Menu command.

MIRRTEXT

MIRRTEXT is an integer that determines whether text is mirrored when the Mirror command is used. If MIRRTEXT is set to 0, text retains its direction and is mirrored but readable. This variable defaults to 1.

ORTHOMODE

This toggle turns Ortho mode on and off. ORTHOMODE defaults to 0 (Off).

OSMODE

OSMODE holds values for the object snap modes currently in use. This integer variable defaults to 0.

PDMODE

PDMODE holds the value of the point-entity display. This integer variable defaults to 0.

PDSIZE

PDSIZE is a real number that defines point-entity size. The default value is 0.

PERIMETER

PERIMETER is a real number representing the perimeter computed by the Area, List, or Dblist command. PERIMETER is read-only.

PICKBOX

This integer variable represents object selection target height, in pixels. The default value is 3. PICKBOX is saved in the ACAD.CFG file.

POPUPS

POPUPS is an integer that determines whether dialogue boxes, menu bars, pull-down menus, and icon menus are supported. This variable is read-only. The default value is 1.

QTEXTMODE

This integer holds the value for the Qtext command. If the value is 0 (the default), Qtext is turned off.

RATVMAX

This variable determines the maximum number of vertices per 3Dface.

REGENMODE

REGENMODE holds the integer value for the
Regenauto command. The default value is 1.

SCREENSIZE

This two-dimensional point indicates the current
viewport size in pixels. SCREENSIZE is read-only.

SHADEDGE

This integer variable determines the type of shading
AutoCAD performs with the Shade command. The
possible values for this variable are

0   3Dface shading with no edge highlighting
1   3Dface shading with edges highlighted in the
       background color
2   Simulated hidden-line shading
3   No shading, but any faces drawn are in their
       original colors

SHADEIF

This integer variable stores a value between 0 and 100
that tells AutoCAD what percentage of light reflecting
from an object is diffused lighting.

SKETCHINC

SKETCHINC is a real number specifying the Sketch
mode increment value. The default value is 0.1

SKPOLY

This integer variable determines whether lines or
polylines are created during Sketch mode. The default
value is 0.

SNAPANG

SNAPANG is a real number indicating the snap/grid
rotation angle for the current viewport. This variable
defaults to 0. A change to this variable is not reflected in
the displayed grid and axis until the screen is redrawn.

SNAPBASE

This two-dimensional value specifies the snap/grid
origin point for the current viewport. A change to this
variable is not reflected in the displayed grid and axis
until the screen is redrawn. The default value is 0,0.

SNAPISOPAIR

This integer variable represents the isoplane currently in use. The default value is 0.

SNAPMODE

This integer variable toggles Snap mode on and off. The default is 0, meaning Snap is turned off.

SNAPSTYL

SNAPSTYL holds the integer value for Snap style. Standard style is 0; isometric is 1. The default is 0.

SNAPUNIT

SNAPUNIT is a two-dimensional point indicating the Snap spacing. A change to this variable is not reflected in the displayed grid and axis until the screen is redrawn. The default value is 1,1.

SPLFRAME

This integer value controls the display of spline frames. SPLFRAME defaults to 0.

SPLINESEGS

This integer indicates the number of line segments to be generated for each spline patch. The default is 8.

SPLINETYPE

This integer controls the type of spline curve to be generated by the Pedit Spline subcommand:

5   Quadratic B-spline
6   Cubic B-spline

The default value is 6.

SURFTAB1

This integer value represents the number of tabulations to be generated for Rulesurf and Tabsurf, and the mesh density in M direction for Revsurf and Edgesurf. SURFTAB1 defaults to 6.

SURFTAB2

This integer variable represents the mesh density in N direction for Revsurf and Edgesurf. SURFTAB2 defaults to 6.

SURFTYPE

The SURFTYPE integer variable determines the type of surface fitting to be performed by Pedit Smooth. The following values are possible:

5   Quadratic B-spline surface
6   Cubic B-spline surface
8   Bezier surface

The default value is 6.

SURFU

SURFU holds the integer value for the M-direction density of meshes defined by the 3Dmesh command. This variable defaults to 6.

SURFV

SURFV holds the integer value for the N-direction density of meshes defined by 3Dmesh command. This variable defaults to 6.

TARGET

TARGET is a three-dimensional point (0,0,0) representing the location of the target set with Dview command. This variable is read-only.

TDCREATE

This real-number variable represents the time and date of drawing creation. TDCREATE is read-only.

TDINDWG

TDINDWG is a real number that represents total editing time. This variable is read-only.

TDUPDATE

TDUPDATE is a real number that stores the time and date of the last update or save. TDUPDATE is read-only.

TDUSRTIMER

This real number represents the user elapsed time. TDUSRTIMER is read-only.

TEMPPREFIX

TEMPPREFIX is a directory name (text string) configured for placement of temporary files. This variable is read-only.

TEXTEVAL

The value of this variable determines how literally text is taken. If the value is 0, any responses to text prompts are taken literally. If the value is 1, any text starting with (or ! is evaluated as an AutoLISP expression.

TEXTSIZE

TEXTSIZE sets the height for new text entities (default of 0.2) drawn in the current text style. If the Text or Dtext commands have been used, this real-number value defaults to the height of the last text string entered.

TEXTSTYLE

TEXTSTYLE is a string containing the name of the current text style. This variable is read-only.

THICKNESS

This real-number variable represents the current three-dimensional thickness The default value is 0.

TILEMODE

This integer number determines whether AutoCAD viewports display entities in model space or in paper space. A value of 0 means that AutoCAD displays and functions in paper space, while a value of 1 causes AutoCAD to work in model space.

TRACEWID

TRACEWID is a real number representing the default trace width. The default value is 0.05.

UCSFOLLOW

If this integer variable is set to 1, AutoCAD allows automatic viewing of plan view for a new UCS. The default is 0.

UCSICON

This integer controls the visibility and location of the UCS icon. The default value of 1 means the icon is visible in all active viewports.

UCSNAME

This variable holds a text string representing the name of the current UCS. UCSNAME is read-only.

UCSORG

UCSORG is a three-dimensional point that holds the origin of the current UCS in World coordinates. The default is 0,0,0. This variable is read-only.

UCSXDIR

This three-dimensional point locates the X-direction of the current UCS. The default is 0,0,0. UCSXDIR is read-only.

UCSYDIR

This three-dimensional point locates the Y-direction of the current UCS. The default is 0,0,0. This variable is read-only.

UNITMODE

This toggle variable controls how feet and inches are displayed. The following values are accepted:

0   Feet and inches are displayed as they have been in the past (for example, 1'-2 3/4").

1   Feet and inches are displayed as they are allowed to be input (for example, 1'2-3/4").

USERI1-5

This setting contains five integer variables for storage and retrieval of integer values (intended for use by third-party developers).

USERR1-5

This setting contains five real-number variables for storage and retrieval of real numbers (intended for use by third-party developers).

VIEWCTR

VIEWCTR is a three-dimensional point (X,Y,Z) representing the center of the view in the current viewport in UCS coordinates. VIEWCTR is read-only.

VIEWDIR

This three-dimensional point (X,Y,Z) represents the viewing direction of the current viewport in World coordinates. The VIEWDIR variable is read-only. It defaults to 0,0,1.

VIEWMODE

VIEWMODE sets the viewing mode for the current viewport. This integer defaults to 0 (Off), but may be set to the sum of the following:

1   Perspective view active
2   Front clipping on
4   Back clipping on
8   UCS follow mode on
16 Front clip not at eye

If on, FRONTZ (the front clipping distance) determines the front clipping plane. If off, FRONTZ is ignored and the front clipping plane is set to pass through the camera point. (Vectors behind the camera are not displayed.) This flag is ignored by FRONTZ if front clipping bit (2) is off.

VIEWSIZE

VIEWSIZE is a real number (the default is 9) representing the height of the view in the current viewport in drawing units. This variable is read-only.

VIEWTWIST

This real-number variable contains the current view-twist angle used by the Dview command. This variable is read-only.

VSMAX

VSMAX is a three-dimensional point representing the upper right corner of the current viewport's "virtual screen" in UCS coordinates. VSMAX is read-only.

VSMIN

VSMIN is a three-dimensional point (the default is 0,0,0) representing the lower left corner of the current viewport's "virtual screen" in UCS coordinates. This variable is read-only.

WORLDUCS

If WORLDUCS is set to 1 (the default), the current UCS is the same as the World Coordinate System. If this variable is set to 0, the current UCS is not the same as the World Coordinate System. This integer variable is read-only.

WORLDVIEW

Normally, View and Vpoint command input is relative
to the current UCS. If this integer variable is set to 1, the
current UCS is changed to the World Coordinate System
for the duration of a Dview or Vpoint command. This
variable is read-only and defaults to a value of 0.

RESPONSE SUMMARY

When you enter a command in AutoCAD, you are often
prompted for additional responses or information. This
section is a quick reminder of possible responses to the
prompts produced when you use AutoCAD commands.
If no additional information is included under a
command, then no additional options are available.

'(Apostrophe)	*Identifies the next command as transparent*
Aperture	*Sets the aperture box size in object snap modes*
Arc	*Draws an arc segment*
A	Angle
C	Center point
D	Starting direction
E	End point
L	Length of chord
R	Radius
Return	(As reply to Start point: prompt) Sets start point and direction at end of last line or arc
Area	*Calculates the area of an object*
A	Add mode
S	Subtract mode
E	Compute area of circle or polyline
Array	*Makes multiple copies of entities*
P	Polar array
R	Rectangular array

Attdef		Creates an attribute definition that controls various aspects of textual information assigned to a block
	I	Control visibility
	C	Control accessibility
	V	Control verification
	P	Control preset mode

Attdisp		Overrides the default visibility setting for all attributes
	ON	Make all attributes visible
	OFF	Make all attributes invisible
	N	Normal visibility

Attedit		Enables you to edit attributes

Attext		Extracts attribute information from the current drawing
	C	Comma-delimited format
	S	Space-delimited format
	D	Drawing Interchange File format
	E	Select particular entities

Audit		Verifies the integrity of a drawing file from within the Drawing Editor
	Y	Fix the errors that are found
	N	Report any errors found, but do not fix them

Axis		Sets up an axis of tick marks on the bottom and right side of the drawing
	ON	Turn on axis
	OFF	Turn off axis
	S	Set axis to current snap value
	A	Change X-Y values
	number	Set tick spacing
	numberX	Set tick spacing to multiple of snap spacing

Base		Specifies the insertion point of the current drawing

Blipmode		Toggles blips on and off
	ON	Turn on marker blips
	OFF	Turn off marker blips

Block	*Creates an object from existing entities*
?	List names of defined blocks
Break	*Removes parts of an entity or separates an entity into segments*
F	Respecify first point
Chamfer	*Connects two lines with a new line segment*
D	Set distances
P	Chamfer polyline
Change	*Modifies entities*
P	Change properties
C	Change color
LA	Change layer
LT	Change linetype
T	Change thickness
Chprop	*Modifies the properties of entities*
C	Change color
LA	Change layer
LT	Change linetype
T	Change thickness
Circle	*Draws a circle*
2P	Specify 2 endpoints of diameter
3P	Specify 3 points on circumference
D	Enter diameter rather than radius
TTR	Specify two tangent points and radius
Color	*Sets the color of new entities*
number	Entity color number
name	Entity color name
BYBLOCK	Floating entity color
BYLAYER	Match layer's color
Copy	*Copies selected objects*
M	Make multiple copies
Dblist	*Lists information about all the entities in a drawing*

Ddatte	*Allows attribute editing by means of a dialogue box*
Ddedit	*Edits both text and attribute definitions by means of a dialogue box*
Ddemodes	*Allows layer-setting changes by means of a dialogue box*
Ddlmodes	*Changes layer properties by means of a dialogue box*
Ddrmodes	*Sets drawing aids by means of a dialogue box*
Dducs	*Controls the User Coordinate System (UCS) by means of a dialogue box*
Delay	*Delays execution of the next command in a script*
Dim, Dim1	*Sets dimensioning mode*
Dist	*Calculates the distance between two points*
Divide	*Divides an entity into equal parts*
B	Use specified block as marker
Donut or Doughnut	*Inserts a solid filled ring in the drawing*
Dragmode	*Modifies dragging*
ON	Turn on dragmode
OFF	Turn off dragmode
A	Auto mode
Dtext	*Draws text dynamically*
(See Text command)	
Dview	*Displays parallel or perspective views*
CA	Select camera angle
CL	Set clipping planes
D	Set distance; turn on perspective

H	Remove hidden lines
OFF	Turn off perspective
PA	Pan drawing
PO	Specify camera and target points
TA	Rotate target point
TW	Twist view
U	Undo
X	Exit
Z	Zoom

Dxbin   Loads binary files produced by programs such as AutoShade

Dxfin   Loads a Drawing Interchange File

Dxfout   Creates a Drawing Interchange File for the current drawing

E	Select specific entities
B	Specify binary file for output

Edgesurf   Constructs a Coons surface patch (a polygon mesh bounded on four sides by entities you select)

Elev   Controls placement of the current X-Y construction plane on the Z axis

Ellipse   Draws ellipses

C	Specify center
R	Rotate ellipse around first axis
I	Draw isometric circle

End   Saves the drawing; exits to the Main Menu

Erase   Removes entities from a drawing

Explode   Separates a block into its original entities

Extend   Extends entities to a boundary

U	Undo the last extension

Files   Permits you to perform limited system operations while still in AutoCAD

Fill

	Controls filling of polylines and solids
ON	Fill solids and wide polylines
OFF	Outline solids and wide polylines

Fillet

	Trims or extends two entities and places a fillet between them
P	Fillet polyline
R	Set fillet radius

Filmroll

Generates a file used for rendering by AutoShade

Graphscr

Switches a single-screen system from text display to graphics display

Grid

	Sets up a rectangular array of reference points within the drawing limits
ON	Turn on grid
OFF	Turn off grid
S	Default grid to snap setting
A	Change X-Y values
number	Set X-Y values
numberX	Set spacing to multiple of snap spacing

Handles

	Controls the system variable for unique identifiers for entities
ON	Assign handles to all entities
DESTROY	Discard all entity handles

Hatch

	Performs hatching
name	Use hatch pattern "name" from library file
U	Use simple user-defined hatch pattern
?	List names of available hatch patterns

The name and U options can be followed by a comma and hatch style from the following list:

I	Ignore style
N	Normal style
O	Hatch outermost portion only

Help or ?	*Provides on-line documentation*
Hide	*Removes hidden lines*
Id	*Returns the coordinates of a point*
Igesin	*Loads Initial Graphics Exchange Standard (IGES) format files*
Igesout	*Converts the current drawing to an IGES format and outputs the data to a new file*
Insert	*Inserts previously defined block*
name	Load block file *name*
name=f	Create block name from file *f*
*name	Retain individual part entities
?	List names of defined blocks
C	Specify corner of scale
XYZ	Ready Insert for X, Y, and Z scales
~	Display a file dialogue box
Isoplane	*Changes orientation of the crosshairs when working in isometrics*
L	Left plane
R	Right plane
T	Top plane
Return	Toggle to next plane
Layer	*Creates and modifies layers*
C*c*	Set specified layers to color *c*
F*a,b*	Freeze layers *a* and *b*
L*t*	Set specified layers to linetype *t*
M*a*	Make *a* the current layer
N*a,b*	Create new layers *a* and *b*
ON*a,b*	Turn on layers *a* and *b*
OFF*a,b*	Turn off layers *a* and *b*
S*a*	Set current layer to layer *a*
T*a,b*	Thaw layers *a* and *b*
?	List layers, colors, and linetypes
Limits	*Controls drawing size*

2 points	Set lower left and upper right drawing limits
ON	Turn on limits checking
OFF	Turn off limits checking

Line	*Draws a straight line*
Return	Start at end of previous line or arc (as reply to From point: prompt)
C	Close polygon (as reply to To point: prompt)
U	Undo segment (as reply to To point: prompt)

Linetype	*Creates, loads, and sets linetypes*
?	List available linetypes
C	Create linetype
L	Load linetype
S	Set linetype for current entity to be drawn

The following suboptions are available if you select the S option:

name	Specify the linetype to use when drawing new entities
BYBLOCK	The linetype of block entities defaults to the layer on which the block is inserted
BYLAYER	Linetype defaults to the setting for the current layer
?	List the linetypes currently in use in the drawing

List	*Lists entity information*

Load	*Loads shape and font files*
?	List loaded shape files

Ltscale	*Changes the scale of linetypes*

Measure	*Measures a distance, placing points or markers at intervals*
B	Use specified block as marker

Menu	*Loads a new menu file for pull-down, screen, tablet, and button menus*

Minsert	*Makes multiple inserts of a block*
name	Load block file *name* and form a rectangular array
name=f	Create block name from file *f* and form a rectangular array
?	List names of defined blocks
C	Specify corner of scale
XYZ	Indicate use of X, Y, Z values
~	Display dialogue box for file-name entry
Mirror	*Reflects entities on an axis*
Move	*Moves entities in the drawing*
Mslide	*Makes a slide of a drawing or part of a drawing*
Mspace	*Switches the current viewport to model space*
Multiple	*Repeats another command until canceled*
Mview	*Treats viewports as entities*
ON	Turn on any selected viewports
OFF	Turn off selected viewports
Hideplot	Removes hidden lines from selected viewports during plotting from paper space
Fit	Create one viewport that fits the current paper space view
2	Create 2 viewports
3	Create 3 viewports
4	Create 4 viewports
Restore	Recreate a previously saved viewport configuration
2 points	Create a viewport inside the area specified by two points
Offset	*Creates a parallel entity*
number	Specify offset distance
T	Specify point through which offset curve will pass
Oops	*Undoes last group erasure*

Ortho	*Restricts user to horizontal or vertical movement of the cursor*
ON	Turn on horizontal/vertical constraint
OFF	Turn off horizontal/vertical constraint

Osnap	*Sets global object snap modes*
CEN	Center of arc or circle
END	Closest endpoint of arc or line
INS	Insertion point of text, block, or shape
INT	Intersection of arc, circle, or line
MID	Midpoint of arc or line
NEA	Point nearest crosshairs on entity
NOD	Node (point)
NON	None; cancel object snap mode
PER	Perpendicular to arc, circle, or line
QUA	Quadrant mode of arc or circle
QUI	Quick mode
TAN	Tangent to arc or circle

Pan	*Enables you to move around in the drawing*

Pedit(2-D, 3-D)	*Permits the editing of polylines*
C	Close open polyline
D	Decurve polyline
E	Edit vertex
F	Fit curve to polyline (not in 3-D)
J	Join to polyline (not in 3-D)
O	Open polyline
S	Use vertices as frame for spline curve
U	Undo
W	Set uniform width for polyline (not in 3-D)
X	Exit

Options for vertex editing:

B	Set first vertex for break
G	Go
I	Insert new vertex after current vertex
M	Move current vertex
N	Make next vertex current

P	Make previous vertex current
R	Regenerate
S	Set first vertex for straighten
T	Set tangent direction (not in 3-D)
W	Set new width for following segment (not in 3-D)
X	Exit vertex editing; cancel break or straighten

Pedit (Meshes) *Permits editing of polygon meshes*

D	Desmooth; restore original
E	Edit vertex
M	Open or close mesh in M direction
N	Open or close mesh in N direction
S	Fit a smooth surface
U	Undo
X	Exit

Options for vertex editing:

D	Move down to previous vertex in M direction
L	Move left to previous vertex in N direction
M	Reposition vertex
N	Move to next vertex
P	Move to previous vertex
R	Move right to next vertex in N direction
RE	Redisplay polygon
U	Move up to next vertex in M direction
X	Exit vertex editing

Pface *Generates a polygon mesh of arbitrary topology, not necessarily composed of four-sided faces*

Plan *Provides a plan view of the drawing relative to the current UCS, a specified UCS, or the WCS*

C	Display plan view of current UCS
U	Display plan view of specified UCS
W	Display plan view of WCS

Pline		Draws polylines
	H	Set new half-width
	U	Undo last Pline command
	W	Set new line width
	Return	Exit

Options for line mode:

	A	Change to arc mode
	C	Close with straight segment
	L	Enter previous segment length

Options for arc mode:

	A	Angle
	CE	Center point
	CL	Close with arc segment
	D	Starting direction
	L	Length of chord; switch to line mode
	R	Radius
	S	Second point of three-point arc

Plot		Plots a drawing on a pen plotter

Point		Inserts point entities into a drawing

Polygon		Draws polygons
	E	Specify edge of polygon
	C	Circumscribe
	I	Inscribe

Prplot		Sends a plot to a printer that accepts graphics information

Pspace		Switches from model space to paper space

Purge		Cleans up the drawing database by removing unused entities
	A	Purge all unused, named objects
	B	Purge unused blocks
	LA	Purge unused layers
	LT	Purge unused linetypes
	SH	Purge unused shapes
	ST	Purge unused text styles

Qtext		Replaces text with a box

ON	Turn on quick-text mode
OFF	Turn off quick-text mode

Quit   *Ends the editing session and returns to the Main Menu without saving changes to the drawing*

Redefine   *Enables you to restore the standard AutoCAD commands to their original definitions*

Redo   *Reverses an Undo command*

Redraw   *Redraws entities on-screen*

Redrawall   *Redraws all viewports at one time*

Regen   *Regenerates the drawing*

Regenall   *Regenerates all viewports*

Regenauto   *Limits automatic regeneration*
ON	Enable automatic regeneration
OFF	Disable automatic regeneration

Rename   *Renames entities*
B	Rename block
D	Rename dimension style
LA	Rename layer
LT	Rename linetype
S	Rename text style
U	Rename UCS
VI	Rename view
VP	Rename viewport

Resume   *Continues an interrupted script file*

Revsurf   *Generates a surface of revolution by rotating an outline around an axis*

Rotate   *Rotates the entities in a drawing*
R	Rotate to referenced angle

Rscript   *Permits repetition of a script file*

Rulesurf	*Creates a ruled surface between two curves, lines, points, arcs, circles, or polylines*
Save	*Saves changes made to the drawing, without returning to the Main Menu*
Scale	*Scales what you have drawn*
R	Scale to referenced length
Script	*Executes a script file in the Drawing Editor*
Select	*Creates a selection set for use in subsequent commands*
Setvar	*Accesses system variables*
?	List any specified system variables
Sh	*Provides partial access to the operating system*
Shape	*Inserts shapes in the drawing*
?	List shape names
Shell	*Provides full access to the operating system*
Sketch	*Permits freehand drawing*
C	Connect new segments to existing segments
E	Erase
P	Raise or lower pen
Q	Exit Sketch mode without saving
R	Save without exiting
X	Save and exit
.	Draw line to current point
Snap	*Locks you into an invisible grid*
number	Set alignment
ON	Turn on snap mode
OFF	Turn off snap mode
A	Change X-Y spacing
R	Rotate snap grid
S	Select standard or isometric style

Solid	*Draws solid rectilinear and triangular areas*
Status	*Displays drawing information*
Stretch	*Changes entities while retaining connections with other entities or points*
Style	*Loads text fonts into a drawing*
?	List text styles
Tablet	*Controls use and layout of the tablet*
ON	Turn on tablet mode
OFF	Turn off tablet mode
CAL	Calibrate tablet
CFG	Configure tablet for tablet menus
Tabsurf	*Creates a tabulated 3-D surface*
Text	*Places text in a drawing*
J	Prompt for justification options
S	Select text style
A	Align text between two points
C	Center text horizontally
F	Fit text between two points
M	Center text horizontally and vertically
R	Right-justify text
BL	Justify text at bottom left
BC	Justify text at bottom center
BR	Justify text at bottom right
ML	Justify text at middle left
MC	Justify text at middle center
MR	Justify text at middle right
TL	Justify text at top left
TC	Justify text at top center
TR	Justify text at top right
Textscr	*Flips to the text screen on a single-screen system*
Time	*Keeps track of time spent in a drawing*
D	Display time
ON	Turn on timer

OFF	Turn off timer
R	Reset timer

Trace   *Draws a line of a specific width*

Trim   *Trims entities back to a boundary*
U   Undoes the last trim

U   *Undoes the most recent command*

Ucs   *Defines or modifies the User Coordinate System*
D   Delete specified UCS
E   Use existing entity to define UCS
O   Define new UCS by moving origin of current UCS
P   Make previous UCS current
R   Restore a saved UCS
S   Save current UCS
V   Define new UCS with Z axis parallel to view direction
W   Set current UCS to World Coordinate System
X   Rotate current UCS around X axis
Y   Rotate current UCS around Y axis
Z   Rotate current UCS around Z axis
ZA   Define new UCS with specified origin and positive Z axis
3   Define new UCS with specified origin, positive X axis, and positive Y axis
?   List saved UCSs

Ucsicon   *Controls the User Coordinate System icon that appears at the bottom of a drawing*
A   Change icon in all viewports
N   Display icon in lower left corner of screen
OR   Display icon at origin of current UCS
OFF   Turn off icon
ON   Turn on icon

Undefine   *Defines normal AutoCAD command to LISP routines*

Undo	*Reverses the effect of previous commands and provides control over the undo feature*
number	Undo specified number of commands
A	Control treatment of menu selections
B	Undo to previous mark
C	Toggle undo feature off and on
E	End undo group
G	Group commands
M	Mark a place in undo information
Units	*Sets the display format and precision of drawing units*
View	*Creates views of zoomed work areas*
D	Delete specified view
R	Restore specified view
S	Save current screen display as view
W	Make area in window a view
?	List views
Vports	*Controls the number of ports on the screen at a given time*
D	Delete saved viewport configuration
J	Join two viewports
R	Restore saved viewport
S	Save current viewport
SI	Display single viewport filling the entire graphics area
2	Divide current viewport into 2 viewports
3	Divide current viewport into 3 viewports
4	Divide current viewport into 4 viewports
?	List saved viewports
Viewres	*Controls fast regeneration and the resolution of circles and arcs*
Vplayer	*Controls a layer's visibility within individual viewports*
?	List all layers frozen within a selected viewport
Freeze	Freeze all specified layers within

	selected viewports
Thaw	Thaw all specified layers within selected viewports
Reset	Reset specified layers to their default visibility
Newfrz	Freeze specified layers in any new viewports
Vpvisdflt	Reset the default viewport visibility for existing layers

Vpoint — *Allows you to see your drawing in three dimensions*

R	Select view using rotation angles
Return	Select view using compass and axes
x,y,z	Specify view point

Vslide — *Allows you to view previously created slides*

file	View slide
*file	Load slide for next Vslide command

Wblock — *Creates blocks that can be used in all drawings*

name	Write file name for block
=	Block name is same as file name
*	Write entire drawing
Return	Write specified block

Xbind — *Permanently attaches pieces of an externally referenced file to the current drawing*

Block	Add a block
Dimstyle	Add a dimension style
Layer	Add a layer
Ltype	Add a linetype
Style	Add a text style

Xref — *Allows you to attach other AutoCAD drawings without making them permanent within the current drawing*

Attach	Attach an externally referenced file to the drawing
Bind	Make an externally referenced file a permanent part of the drawing

Detach	Permanently remove any externally referenced files from the drawing
Path	Specify a new path to locate an externally referenced file
Reload	Update any externally referenced files within the drawing
?	List all externally referenced files that are a part of the current drawing

Zoom	*Magnifies or condenses the screen image*
number	Zoom by a factor from original scale
numberX	Zoom by a factor from current scale
numberXP	Zoom by a factor relative to paper space
A	All
C	Specify new center point
D	Dynamic
E	Extents
L	Set new lower left corner
P	Return to previous screen
V	Zoom to virtual screen maximum
W	Place window around work area

3Dface	*Draws three-dimensional flat planes*
I	Make following edge invisible

3Dmesh	*Creates a three-dimensional polygon mesh*

3Dpoly	*Draws three-dimensional polylines*
C	Close polyline
U	Undo last endpoint
Return	Exit